The Need for Freedom: Markets as Solutions to Global Poverty

Eben Macdonald

Clink Street

Published by Clink Street Publishing 2022

Copyright © 2022

First edition.

The author asserts the moral right under the Copyright, Designs and Patents Act 1988 to be identified as the author of this work.

All rights reserved. No part of this publication may be reproduced, stored in a retrieval system or transmitted, in any form or by any means without the prior consent of the author, nor be otherwise circulated in any form of binding or cover other than that with which it is published and without a similar condition being imposed on the subsequent purchaser.

ISBN:
978-1-914498-23-7 - paperback
978-1-914498-24-4 - ebook

CHAPTER 1

The Importance of Economic Growth

As I write, the World Bank has recently released grim statistics. In 2020, up to 88 million people fell into extreme poverty worldwide.[1] The global Sars-Cov-19 pandemic forced many nations to adopt strict lockdown measures. Businesses were prevented from operating; schools were prevented from teaching students face-to-face and ordinary life became suppressed. Adhering to strict social regulations, such as mask wearing in public, has become routine and a feature of everyday life.

These regulations were supported to curb the spread of the virus. However, too little attention is paid to the horrendous social and economic consequences borne by the most vulnerable in society. A multitude of social ills, ranging from violence against women to drug addiction to unemployment, have all been exacerbated.

In November 2020, the pharmaceutical company Pfizer announced the development of an mRNA vaccine, which governments have adopted to reduce the impact of the virus.[2] Vaccination rates are only sufficient in richer countries, while they lag significantly in poorer ones: as of July 2021, 27.1 percent of the global population has received at least one dose of any Covid-19 vaccines. This varies considerably depending on income levels. 'Low-income' countries have vaccination rates of 1.1 percent on average.[3]

Increasing vaccination rates has been promoted to alleviate burdens on social infrastructure. Discussing how to increase vaccination uptake is not the point of this book. I aim to explore what can effectively sustain long-term economic recovery from the severe recessions induced by lockdowns. Specifically, I want to prescribe one kind of medicine: economic liberalism. Later chapters will define this idea and explore the economic theory behind what it is and why it works. In this chapter, however, we shall explore the economic phenomenon which is the most closely associated with poverty reduction: economic growth.

Economic growth refers to increase in the total economic value produced per person in a population. The most popular statistical metric for this is gross domestic product (GDP) per capita. The total value of all goods and services produced within a country is divided by the total size of the population, to give a measure of a peoples' material standard of living. Of course, income is influenced by national cost of living, which is why GDP per capita statistics are adjusted for purchasing price parity (PPP), to improve the accuracy of income measurements.

Across the world, there is enormous variation in GDP per capita, ranging from $3000 in the war-torn Democratic Republic of the Congo to $129,000 in oil-rich Qatar.[4]

Politicians in developed Western countries tend to dismiss GDP per capita as an irrelevant statistic; it is easily understood and used by journalists to attack the perceived failures of governments' economic agendas, but in fact does not correlate with and reflect peoples' true standard of living. In a 1968 speech at the University of Kansas, then-presidential candidate Robert Kennedy said the following of GDP: "It measures neither our wit nor our courage, neither our wisdom nor our learning, neither our compassion nor our devotion to our country, it measures everything in short, except that which makes life worthwhile."[5] These things include, according to Kennedy, health, education, and culture. However, GDP strongly correlates with health, social, and educational indicators in the developing world; it is logical that as average material living standards rise, access to social infrastructure improves. Thinkers argue that in already-rich countries, economic growth can no longer have an impact on median living standards, nor 'trickle down' to benefit the poor. Whether this is correct or not (it isn't), is irrelevant. This book is concerned with poverty in the developing nations only, which economic growth is most certainly able to alleviate. Poverty in rich countries enjoys the material benefits economic growth provides, albeit being highly influenced by broader social welfare policy. In the United States, for example, 46 percent of poor families own a house, 76 percent own a refrigerator and almost 75 percent own a car.[6] These are possessions which are unheard of in households of the extremely globally poor.

The most important statistics to take note of are on the relationship between per capita income and the poverty rate.[7] Economists have identified what's known as a 'hockey-stick correlation' between the two. At low levels of income, as incomes rise even sightly, poverty drops considerably. Beyond a certain point, extreme poverty – defined as income below $1.90 a day – has already been eradicated, so additional increases in income are not important.

The income–poverty correlation can be tested further. We can investigate how well changes in per capita income track with changes in poverty. In 2010, economists Xavier Sala-i-Martin and Maxim Pinkovskiy collected data on exactly this from sub-Saharan Africa.[8] The correlation they identified between the percentage of the population living below $1.90 a day and GDP per capita was noticeably strong – when incomes stagnate or decline, as they did in the region from the 1970s to 1990s, the poverty rate flatlines or rises. When they rise, however, the poverty rate diminishes.

Of course, this poverty line is incredibly low and relying on it as the only possible metric fails to recognise that incomes above this line are not at all comfortable. We still express concern for people living below $5 a day. Nevertheless, being lifted above the $1.90 a day threshold would translate into dramatically higher living standards for almost a billion people.

The Need for Freedom

Economic growth can alleviate absolute poverty at much higher thresholds too. A simple way to test this empirically is to measure the income growth rates of the poorest segments of society and see if those rates correlate with overall income growth. The answer is an emphatic 'yes'. The most notable study of this comes from the economists David Dollar and Aart Kraay, who authored a 2001 paper *Growth is Good for the Poor*. Having examined a large dataset of 92 countries, they wrote: "Average incomes of the poorest fifth of society rise proportionately with average incomes."[9]

The 'coefficient of determination' (also known as 'the correlation squared') measures how much of the variation in the dependent variable in a dataset can be attributed to the independent variable. A coefficient of 1 suggests that 100 percent of the variation can be attributed to the independent variables; 0 suggests that none can whatsoever and is therefore statistically irrelevant. Their paper found a 0.88 correlation squared coefficient between average income and the incomes of the bottom quintile of the income scale. It also discovered a highly substantial 0.49 coefficient between average income *growth* and the income growth of that socioeconomic segment. Some analysts worry that economic growth benefits the rich more than the poor and produces increases in income inequality (probably because higher-income jobs, such as CEOs, are seen as capturing most of the increase in value from production). However, Dollar and Kraay's study found no association whatsoever between annual growth in average income and change in income inequality. The OECD admits that the relationship between growth and rising inequality has been "far from uniform."[10]

These determining coefficients – 0.88 and 0.49 – are immensely strong. If we put aside the 'correlation does not necessarily imply causation' maxim for one moment and assume that there is a genuine connection (positive or negative) between growth and absolute poverty alleviation, these data would strongly suggest it is positive.

Dollar and Kraay replicated their findings in 2013, showing once again that economic growth is still by far the greatest reducer of poverty and driver of the incomes of poor quintiles.[11] In a 2014 article, the two economists wrote that 90 percent of the variation in the change of 'social welfare' (a measure of economic equitability and living standards) can be attributed to change in per capita income of 117 countries over a 42-year period.[12] Dollar and Kraay's research is corroborated by separate research papers. A 2003 study by Richard Adams examined 50 countries and found that a 10 percent increase in mean income is associated with a 26 percent reduction in the proportion of the population living below $1 a day.[13] In a 2015 report, the World Bank took data of a big group of countries over the period 2006 to 2011. In doing so, they discovered a powerful relationship between the growth rates of average incomes, and the growth rates in income of the poorest 40 percent of the population.[14]

Regardless of if average economic growth increases income inequality – for which there is little evidence anyway – it is obvious that it improves the living standards of society's less fortunate in absolute terms, not simply relative terms, which ought to be the real moral objective of any social system.

The World Bank report argues that to end world poverty, substantial levels of economic growth would be required. This book will argue that such are certainly achievable, if developing nations implement the correct economic policies.

It is typical for many to attribute to the large reductions in poverty which have occurred in middle- and lower-income countries to increased government social welfare spending, instead of economic growth. The evidence for this is extraordinarily weak. In 2018, researchers conducted a meta-analysis of 19 studies done on the relationship between welfare spending and poverty reduction. In their own words, "we find no clear evidence that higher government spending has played a large role in reducing poverty in low- and middle-income countries". The relationship between welfare spending and

The Need for Freedom

poverty was found to be *more* negative in already more developed economies, such as in Eastern Europe and Central Asia, than in the least developed ones, like in sub-Saharan Africa.[15]

Fine, you might say, economic growth can be shown to increase a population's material welfare. But what about all the other important factors that define living standards – like health and education – which, as Kennedy remarked, make 'life worthwhile'? Of course, people become healthier, better educated, and more societally cohesive as economic growth occurs. As incomes rise, more families can afford to send their children to school, access to and the quality of medicine increases, the quality and safety of housing improves, and political stability even increases. In the same way GDP per capita strongly predicts a country's poverty rate, it can also predict a host of other social variables. These include life expectancy, infant mortality, number of deaths from diseases, average years of schooling, life satisfaction and even cultural indicators, such as how much people trust one another.[16]

Some economists would object to my interpretations of data offered above. First, the richer a country becomes, the weaker these relationships become. This is completely true. For example, after GDP per capita exceeds $20,000, the relationship between per capita income and life expectancy becomes significantly weaker. However, this is not a relevant argument: this book is investigating the solution to poverty found in developing economies only – if economic growth becomes incapable of improving social indicators beyond a certain point, then so be it. A second objection might be that while economic variables might strongly predict social ones, they do not do so as strongly as others might. For example, health expenditure per capita also strongly predicts life expectancy. The truth is government expenditure on anything is contingent on economic growth. Governments cannot spend much on healthcare if a stagnant economy won't yield the revenues to pay for that. This would explain the fairly linear association between GDP per capita and health expenditure per capita.[17] Admittedly, this relationship deteriorates almost completely after $45,000. But only very developed economies are behind the ruining of this correlation – which are irrelevant to our study. Among emerging markets, average income is powerfully associated with what governments are able to spend on healthcare. A separate study by the World Bank and the World Health Organisation (WHO) found a huge correlation between GDP per capita and the Universal Health Care Index, which measures the population's access to healthcare.[18]

Interestingly, historical case studies show that the greatest improvements in a population's health standards occur before governments make conscious efforts to increase access to healthcare facilities. To give one example, between 1871 and 1951 British life expectancy rose from 41.4 years for males and 44.6 years for females to 66.4 years and 71.5 years, respectively. Yet, it was only in 1947 that the government established universal access to the National Health Service. Since then, the rise in life expectancy has in fact slowed.[19] This is not to say that this intervention has *caused* life expectancy to slow. It is simply to make the point that improvement in health indicators is contingent on income growth and the elevation of material living standards, and governments typically only begin spending money on public services once they have the resources to do so.

Education, on the other hand, is a more complex matter. It is true that per capita income predicts how educated the population is, and how much is spent on education per capita. However, here reverse causality may prove to be a genuine issue: it is just as plausible that spending on education increases per capita income, not the other way around, because the population is given the essential human capital with which to participate in the economy and behave productively.[20] It is conceivable that there is a reciprocal relationship between educational access and per capita income growth: at first, access to education increases only because per capita living standards rise. This in turn fuels greater growth in per capita income, which then further increases access to education.

Some worry economic growth is environmentally detrimental. The truth about this is complex; addressing it requires help from the environmental Kuznets curve (EKC). The original Kuznets curve states that with basic stages of economic development, income inequality increases, but once development exceeds a certain threshold, inequality begins to decrease. EKC substitutes environmental quality for income inequality. As countries experience their earliest stages of economic development, environmental quality declines. Beyond a point, however, this turns around, and economic growth comes to be associated with environmental *improvements*.[21] Let's see the empirical evidence for this.

- A study examined the relationship between per capita income and a host of environmental indicators, such as the atmospheric concentrations of sulphur dioxide, nitrogen oxide, carbon dioxide and suspended particles matters (SPM). The turning points for different indicators vary. For SPM and sulphur dioxide, they range from $8000 to $10,300. For nitrogen dioxide, however, they are between $11,200 and $21,800.
- But another study, involving 149 countries over a 30-year period, found that the turning points for SPM and sulphur dioxide are much lower, at $3280 and $3670.
- An examination of 130 countries over the period 1951 to 1986 reviewed the relationship between per capita income and CO_2 emissions specifically. The turning point was found to be much higher, at $34,428.[22]
- Another analysis found that the turning points for tropical deforestation are thankfully very low, at between $800 and $1200, as well with sulphur dioxide, which were between $3800 and $5500.[23]

We have explored the empirical relationship between economic growth, rising living standards, poverty alleviation, and environmental quality. But in any science, including economics, it is necessary to explain the correlations which research finds: *why* does economic growth improves material wellbeing, and a variety of social indicators as a result?

Firstly, as the economy grows, populations' incomes rise. As a result, consumer demand rises, incentivising businesses to invest and innovate. This leads to newer, better quality, and cheaper goods. In a typical Western supermarket, there are varieties of meats, fruits and vegetables, sugary delights, and other products which kings and queens hundreds of years ago would have envied. This in turn fuels more economic growth: if consumers enjoy the benefits of lower prices, they can spend the money they saved elsewhere. Demand for innovation and for business production to rise. The same applies if workers receive higher wages, and more are employed and thus earning an income. Obviously, the innovations which result from economic expansion lead to more economic growth as well. Before, you might have had to use a bicycle to access the marketplace to sell your goods. But now, you have a car. Getting to the marketplace is a ten-minute journey. You are able to sell vastly more products, more frequently. This will certainly improve your material standard of living – and that of all the other millions of people who now own cars.

Secondly, as the economy grows, demand for labour rises. To respond to consumer demands by raising production, businesses need to expand the sizes of their workforces. Economic growth is sometimes associated with rising commodity prices, which is influenced by the mechanism of supply and demand. A 2021 study by the International Monetary Fund (IMF) identified the total growth in commodity prices from 2000 to 2014 in South and Latin America as being strongly associated with the concomitant reductions in poverty and income inequality across the continent.[24] As the paper states, during commodity booms, the demand for labour to support production tends to rise. This puts upward pressure on wages, especially those of unskilled workers.

Thirdly, economic growth improves the overall productive value of labour, and makes productive jobs more dominant in the economy. Once upon a time, most of the workforce laboured away on farms. During the Industrial Revolution, this changed completely: workers migrated to the cities where factories offered significantly higher wages than what they would find on a farm. In fact, in Great Britain, factory wages would be up to double farm wages.[25] In developed nations a negligible portion of the workforce works on works. The mechanisation of agriculture noticeably reduced the need for a substantial workforce on farmland. Not only did this massively increase food abundance, and hence lower costs, it also sent workers to work in much more productive economic sectors, which have provided the goods, services, and infrastructure which define modernity. We certainly tend to associate development with the composition of the economy. While farm labour is virtually non-existent in the rich West, it constitutes much of the workforce in poorer economies.

Finally, a correlate of economic growth is recognised to be the Baumol effect, named after the economist who proposed it in the 1960s, William J. Baumol.[26] There are many jobs which cannot be affected by increases in technological productivity, in contrast to others: a tailor can make vastly more dresses now than a hundred years ago, thanks to better machinery. But a hairdresser today can't cut hair that much faster than they could a hundred years ago. Yet, both professions are significantly better remunerated now than all that time ago. Why? The Baumol Effect states that wage growth will take place in technologically limited sectors of the economy thanks to growth occurring in the more developed ones. Here's how it works: as wages in some sectors rise, workers in other sectors move into them. This causes the labour supply in lower wage parts of the economy, which can't really be affected by technological progress, to become limited. As a result of the laws of supply and demand, wages in these sectors thus increase. Some economists are derided for saying "a rising tide lifts all boats." However, this is true. As wages in already productive sectors rise, wages in more unproductive sectors rise as a result. Economic growth benefits everyone, skilled and unskilled, rich, and poor.

Is it possible to have poverty alleviation without economic growth? The only conceivable way for this to happen would be for governments to spend extraordinary amounts of money on welfare programs (which, as later chapters will find, may have limited impacts on poverty anyway). In a hypothetical zero-growth world, tax revenues would not be rising, while spending most certainly would. This would therefore cause the national debt to rise substantially, and almost inevitably surpass 100 percent of GDP. Debt is financed by bondholders on the assumption that, at maturity, the government borrower will repay them. But in a world of zero-growth, and thus no incoming tax revenues, this could never happen. There would thus be two options: to either default on the debt, in which case, spending would have to be dramatically cut, or pay off the debt with Quantitative Easing (QE), the mass printing of money. This never ends well – usually it ends in massive inflation, which destroys living standards. To sustain government finances, growth is required. The zero-growth-poverty-alleviating utopia hence repeals itself. To spend money, the economy needs to grow. But in the absence of growth, governments can't spend, which ultimately reduces growth through debt, and so forth.

In Chapter 8, we will explore the crippling macroeconomic effects of excessive government spending, which undo the objectives government investment tends to have.

These are the reasons why economic growth reduces poverty and raises overall living standards. Its importance cannot be stressed enough. In the following chapter, we will examine the role of economic growth is raising the living standards of rich Western countries, when they weren't so rich.

CHAPTER 2

When the West Wasn't so Rich

The West didn't always use to have the standard of living it enjoys today. It used to levels of poverty and squalor which are commonly seen in developing world today. In 1870, Western Europe's per capita income was $3301, roughly that of sub-Saharan Africa's in 2016. In the same year, Europe's life expectancy was 36.2 years, almost as low as Africa's was 80 years later. In 1800, the percentage of children dying before the age of five years old was between 30 percent and 60 percent in every single European country. This was a range Africa's child mortality rates did not diminish into until 1950.[1]

Thanks to industrialisation, however, Europe's average standard of living has risen by more than tenfold since 1870.[2] The problems which severely afflict the developing world today – hunger, extreme poverty, child labour, gruellingly long working hours, infant mortality, and low life expectancy – have virtually disappeared in the West.

What deserves credit for this? It is common for the public to attribute these improvements to social welfare programs, labour unions bargaining with employers, and government regulations on businesses to limit 'worker exploitation'. However, as this chapter shall reveal, the greatest improvements in these indicators in the West *preceded* substantial government and union involvement in economic affairs, or simply occurred independently of them – and often, these improvements did not accelerate after union or government involvement in matters increased. The only plausible explanation is that economic growth brought about these advances. Let's look at a bunch of examples: extreme poverty, the presence of child labour, long working hours, workplace deaths.

Extreme Poverty

State-provided social safety nets undeniably serve as bulwarks against poverty to some extent. However, it is a matter of complete conjecture to say that the disappearance of extreme poverty in the West can be attributed to these programs.

In 2010, economic historians at the University of Sussex, Ian Gazeley and Andrew Newell, showed that the most substantial declines in British extreme poverty occurred before the major expansions of the welfare state after the Second World War.

They noted that the most significant decline in poverty occurred in the United Kingdom between 1904 and 1937. It is true that certain welfare programs had been established by the Liberal government in the early 1900s. However, the authors argue that there were essentially two major factors driving this reduction: the decline in family size and the rise in real wages. The decline in family size they attribute mainly to the spread of the contraceptives; the rise in real wages will be attributed by some to labour unions negotiating and bargaining with employers. From 1900 to 1940, UK trade union membership rose considerably, by a factor of three – and during this period, real average weekly wages rose by a total of 41.5 percent. To prove that this growth occurred mainly due to trade union bargaining, we'd have to find that wage growth was slower in the 40 years before 1900, when union membership was much lower. Two pro-union economists, Alejandro Donado and Klaus Wälde, have collected data which goes back before 1900.[4] Unfortunately, their statistics on Britain only go back 1892, eight years before our benchmark. This shouldn't be a problem, so long as we make the plausible assumption that UK trade union membership was substantially lower in 1860, 40 years before 1900, than over the period 1900–1940. In 1892, 10.6 percent of the British workforce was a member of a trade union; there's no reason to believe it was any higher than that in 1860. The next thing to do is measure total real wage growth over that 40-year period. As it turns out, in total wages grew by a total of 48.5 percent over that period.[5] How is it logical to attribute the rise in workers' real living standards which occurred from 1900 to 1940 to collective bargaining, if the rise had been stronger in the previous 40 years, yet with far weaker trade unions? In other words, the sharp reduction in poverty which Gazeley and Newell's study identified as taking place between 1904 and 1937 probably had nothing to do with union bargaining.

Evidence from the United States also informs the discussion on the role labour unions and social welfare programs played in reducing poverty.

When poverty in the United States is talked about, it is common a specific decade is mentioned – the 1960s. In 1960, a young Senator of New York state, John F. Kennedy, was elected president. Inaugurated in 1961, his term was tragically cut short less than three years later, when he was struck by an assassin's bullet. Vice president Lyndon B. Johnson ascended to the presidency. Kennedy had discussed huge investment in social welfare programs, but little increases in spending had occurred under him. Johnson was determined to continue his predecessor's legacy. In his 1964 address to Congress, Johnson announced "This administration today, here, and now, declares unconditional war on poverty in America."[6] On what were known as the Great Society programs, between 1965 and 1970, means-tested welfare spending rose from $77 billion to $145 billion. Many perceive these programs as having been successful. The US poverty rate fell from 19 percent in 1964 to 11.1 percent in 1974.[7] However, the progress against poverty which had taken place in the years preceding 1965 is rarely acknowledged.

Official poverty statistics were only being collected starting in 1958, so poverty estimates before then may suffer problems of reliability. But nevertheless, data do exist, and seem to have strong academic substance. In a voluminous 2004 book, *Poverty in the United States*, researchers showed that between 1949 and 1959, the decade before any welfare programs of the Kennedy–Johnson ambitions were being implemented, the poverty rate declined from 34.9 percent to 21.3 percent. This would suggest that much of the decline in poverty which occurred during the 1960s was simply a continuation of a pre-existing trend.[8]

Yet still, academics have been able to obtain statistics going back even further in time. A 1998 study by the Institute for Research on Poverty gave data starting in 1917.[9] According to them, between 1935 and 1944, the US poverty rate fell from 80 percent to just shy of 20 percent.

This further reinforces the message that most of America's alleviation of poverty took place long before the Great Society programs were initiated. Of course, America did not completely lack a welfare state before 1960. Under the New Deal, Franklin Roosevelt had established a handful of social safety net programs – and poverty declined sharply during Roosevelt's presidency, which lasted from 1933 to 1945. In response to this, a reader of the Institute's paper will find that the decline in poverty, which had been taking place in the early 1930s, accelerated dramatically between 1939 and 1945. Any casual historical observer will notice that this coincides perfectly with the Second World War. Indeed, this war was greatly beneficial to the American economy because the country was at the forefront of answering Allied demand for war products – cars, jeeps, tanks, planes, ships, bullets, and bombs. This high demand produced extraordinary economic growth in the United States. Annual GDP growth averaged at 12.9 percent over this period. This was facilitated by millions of Americans from the underdeveloped, rural Southern states to the industrial Northern ones, where many munitions factories existed.[10] If anything, this provides evidence that economic growth was the most important factor in the reduction of poverty before the 1960s. The paper featuring the graph above admits just this: "Growth in mean income was far and away the most important factor [in the decline in poverty], and its antipoverty effect was reinforced by the decline in inequality."

Besides, the antipoverty impact of Roosevelt's New Deal tends to be vastly overexaggerated. The US government indeed enacted sizeable increases in welfare spending. These were not sufficient to produce remarkable declines in poverty:

> In a time when minimum subsistence was thought to be around $100 per month ($115 by the deflated 1964 official poverty line), the most generous program of the time—the Works Progress Administration—was only paying about $55 per month. No other program paid even half as much.

While most of Roosevelt's social insurance programs were "large in relation to their predecessors," they were "too small to be effective." Another particularly large welfare program initiated by the Roosevelt Administration was Social Security. However Social Security cheques, which were aimed at the elderly, were only being received by one-sixth of Americans aged 65 and older in the year after the war ended.[11]

True, the economy was highly centralised during the war. For example, strict price controls were put in place, as well as rationing programs. It is conceivable, however, that considerable growth would have occurred during the war regardless of whether this had been the case or not, as wartime demand would have led to rapid increases in production anyway. Price controls, for instance, led to shortages of everyday necessities, such as milk, and probably cost jobs in other sectors of the economy.[12]

America's economic miracle continued well after the war. Many economists, such as Paul Krugman, argue that this was driven by high government expenditures and the famous 'G.I. Bill' which transferred military veterans to colleges. There's a problem with this argument. Firstly, after the war, government expenditures fell substantially: from 1944 to 1947, spending fell from 55 to just 16 percent of GDP, a 75 percent decline. The much-celebrated G.I. Bill only transferred 8 percent of former G.I.s from the workplace to college campuses.[13] Besides, as Alan Greenspan and Adrian Woodridge point out, much of the rise in college attendance after the war was due to factors other than the G.I. Bill, such as programs focusing on intellectually competent children and the fact that America "avoided the mistake of turning higher education into a nationalised industry, allowing public and private universities to flourish side by side and encouraging the creation of new sorts of institutions."[14]

It is similarly true that the tax burden was incredibly high during the post-war economic boom. For example, in the 1950s, the top marginal tax rate was an above 90 percent. However, this tax rate only applied to households with incomes higher than $200,000. This meant that only 10,000 households at the time were affected by this rate! (Besides, because of these astronomical rates, there was a significant level of tax avoidance).[15]

There are certainly other factors which could have contributed to the reduction in poverty in America during this period. After all, from 1935 to 1945, the unionisation rate rose by more than threefold, from just over 10 percent to 35 percent. With workers fighting aggressively for higher wages, unions may have served as fundamental weapons against poverty. The objections to this argument are both theoretical and empirical. Firstly, as we have discussed, the reduction in poverty over 1939–1945 was strongly driven by workers migrating to higher wage areas, predominantly from the Southern states to the Northern ones, in order to seek better remunerated employment. This sudden migration occurred thanks to the war, which created massive demand for American labour, and thus higher wages in the relevant industries. The basic laws of economics can explain the economic benefits of America's war economy, and labour unions are not needed for that explanation. However, we can argue that unions were in fact an *obstacle* to the 1939–1945 poverty reduction. To understand this, it is necessary to understand how unions operate on a fundamental level. To raise wages, unions like to tinker with the mechanism of supply and demand. Through limiting the supply of labour in a particular company, the wages paid to the incumbent employees resultantly increase. However, this means that fewer people are able to get a job in the first place and, especially in the context of the 1940s, are likely to remain mired in poverty. Workers can't enjoy the benefits of higher wages if they can't get higher-wage jobs in the first place.

Is there empirical evidence, aside from pure theory, that unions hindered employment growth during this period? There is certainly evidence of a specific group being bullied by labour unions throughout their history: American Blacks were frequently willing to work at lower wages than their white counterparts; and thus, industries were naturally more willing to employ them. This caused great economic anxiety among white workers, who feared they'd be displaced from their jobs, or would have their wages competed down. Therefore, an unignorable function of labour unions was to exclude American Blacks from employment, often by violent means. The historian Paul Moreno observes that white workers feared possible wage competition with Black jobseekers and used labour unions to prevent them from obtaining employment.[16]

It is unlikely that unions played a positive role in America's war economy. They likely had an adverse effect on employment, especially by terrorising and excluding one of America's most vulnerable socioeconomic groups, who were disproportionately affected by poverty.

Did minimum wage laws help alleviate poverty? Established under the 1938 Fair Labour Standards Act, Could they have played any important role in poverty alleviation? Probably not. This minimum wage was very quickly made redundant by strong wage inflation.[17] Anyhow, there is much theoretical and empirical evidence that the minimum wage harms precisely those who it intends to help – low wage, predominantly unskilled, workers. When a minimum floor for labour is imposed, above the productive value of many workers' labour, a big echelon society may be excluded from employment. They tend to be young, uneducated, and are disproportionately racial minorities. The historian Leonard Thomas has found that the concept of a minimum wage had a strong eugenic motivation, to prevent certain racial groups from competing with others in the labour market.[18]

Child Labour

The employment of young children in the labour force persists in the developing world today. It used to be a big issue in Western countries, too. In 1880, 22.9 percent of British boys between 10 and 14 were employed, along with 15.1 percent of girls. In the United States, it was 32.5 percent and 12.2 percent, respectively.[19]

It is easy to look back on historical child labour, and examine modern-day child labour, with horror. It is easy to label it cruel and exploitative. But well-intended philanthropists and political figures let their emotions get the better of them. They thoughtlessly advocate regulations to restrict children's working hours or employment, without considering the possible consequences. In the poor populations of many countries, sending a child to work spells the difference between severe destitution and starvation. As was written in a study by the thinktank International Labour Organized (ILO):[20]

> More robust evidence, controlling for household attributes that accompany income poverty, also points to a strong connection between poverty and child labour. Country studies on child labour, for instance, consistently show that, other things being equal, poor children are more likely to work than their better-off peers.... A growing number of studies drawing on longitudinal or episodic

data also consistently support the view that poverty induces households to rely more on child labour.

The ILO also observes that families tend to rely more on child labour in times of economic hardship:[21]

> Studies in Cambodia... and Tanzania... found that substantially higher proportions of children worked in villages experiencing agriculture-related shocks such as drought, flood and crop failure. A study looking specifically at unemployment in urban Brazil found that adult job loss had a sizeable effect on the likelihood of children dropping out of education and working.... Another study, focusing on the impact of the harsh economic downturn in Venezuela during 2002–03, found that the proportion of children engaged in market work nearly doubled while GDP was falling, and then dropped as the economy recovered.

This should indicate that economic growth is effectively the control knob on many of the world's social and economic problems. If you want to reduce child labour today, you need to achieve reasonably high rates of economic growth.

This was equally true of the undeveloped West. In his 1949 magnum opus, *Human Action*, Austrian economist Ludwig von Mises explained that child labour was a lifeline to poor families:[22]

> It is a distortion of facts to say that the factories carried off the housewives from the nurseries and the kitchen and the children from their play. These women had nothing to cook with and to feed their children. These children were destitute and starving. Their only refuge was the factory. It saved them, in the strict sense of the term, from death by starvation.

Children were not coerced into entering the labour market – they did so because their families absolutely needed them to.

The Need for Freedom

Thus, any attempt to regulate child labour should be taken with great caution. If child labourers' access to the market is cut off, their households will be put in a considerably worse position. There is strong empirical evidence behind this. A 2013 study by economists Prashant Bharadwaj, Leah Lakdawala, and Nicholas Lee examined the long-term consequences of India's Child Labor (Prohibition and Regulation) Act of 1986. Their findings were highly counterintuitive: instead of having its intended effect of reducing child labour, the law had in fact *increased* it. The authors explain that in response to regulation, child labourers' wages tended to decrease. Poorer families have to compensate for this lost income by *utilising more child labour*. The study notes that this increase in child labour has come at the expense of education. In the long run, this will depress workers' development of human capital, which will reduce their life opportunities even further.

The increase in child labour was partly able to occur due to the incompetence of the regulatory authorities. The study explains:

> While enforcement of the 1986 law has been largely weak, it does appear that employers were aware of the law. According to a report by Human Rights Watch, many employers found loopholes to work around the specifics of the law. For example, the report… provides anecdotal evidence on factories contracting with adults to take work home for their children since work at home was allowed under the terms of the law.[23]

Of course, proponents of regulations on child labour rarely consider that government authorities will be inefficient and incompetent at monitoring child labour, so would been unable to reduce it substantially even if they tried.

While child labour prevails in poverty-stricken nations, it no longer exists in the West. What caused its disappearance? There is much research attempting to answer this question, such as by the economic historians Robert Whaples and Clark Nardinelli. Nardinelli observes that rates of child labour in Victorian Britain were in decline before the legislation of the 1820s limiting it was passed. In his own words,

> [W]hile it cannot be denied that legislation reduced child labor in the short run, an economic approach indicates that rising incomes, not factory legislation, was chiefly responsible for the long-term reduction in child labor. As income rise in any economy, child labor declines and the general condition of children improves. As the industrial revolution increased income in Britain (and elsewhere), changing opportunities enabled the typical family to reduce its reliance on the labor of children.[24]

Whaples concentrates his research more on the United States. He notices that child labour had virtually disappeared in the United States long before federal regulations on it were imposed. Between 1880 and 1930, the percentage of 10-to-15-year-old boys in employment fell from 32.5 percent to 6.4 percent – and from 12.2 percent to 2.9 percent for girls. This had all happened comfortably before the 1938 Fair Labor Standards Act, which put considerable restrictions on child employment in the United States.[25]

Of course, state and local governments in America had been placing their own regulations on child labour long before national legislation was implemented, Massachusetts being the earliest state, in 1837. To this, Whaples, responds:[26]

> Most economic historians conclude that this legislation was *not* the primary reason for the reduction and virtual elimination of child labor between 1880 and 1940. Instead, they point out that industrialization and economic growth brought rising incomes, which allowed parents the luxury of keeping their children out of the work force. In addition, child labor rates have been linked to the expansion of

schooling, high rates of return from education, and a decrease in the demand for child labor due to technological changes which increased the skills required in some jobs and allowed machines to take jobs previously filled by children.

In a 1999 study, Carolyn Moehling found that although the employment rates of 13-year-olds declined in states where minimum-age employment laws of 14 had been set, they declined just as much in states where 13-year-olds were covered by such 'symbolic' regulations.[27]

Hopefully, this elucidates the argument that economic growth ended child labour in the West, and economic and income growth are necessary in the developing world to achieve the same. This necessarily explains the highly negative association between GDP per capita and child employment rates across many countries, and why child employment rates have come tumbling down across the world over the decades.[28]

Working Hours

In heavily poor countries, long hours of backbreaking labour are the norm. In Cambodia, for example, the work year takes 2456 hours, as opposed to 1359 in Germany. Once upon a time in England the average worker would toil for 56.9 hours in one week; they'd only take 14 days in one year to enjoy a holiday (now it's 33 days). Of course, working hours also exposed harsh gender inequalities. In 1900, the average American woman over the age of 14 would spend 42.5 hours on home chores; by 2005, that had declined to 27.6 hours.[29]

Thankfully, working hours have declined significantly in the West. A British worker had to labour 56.9 hours a week in 1870; in 2000, it was 40.45 hours.[30] Because working hours can have such a large effect upon the quality of life, it is essential we explain the cause of this decline. As with child labour, many attribute it to government-enforced regulation, but more so to labour unions, who pressured their employers in reducing working hours.

Economists across the political spectrum accept that increasing worker productivity is the best way to reduce working hours (and in general raise workers' living standards) – in other words, as counterintuitive as it may seem, the more output per worker there is, the fewer hours workers work. In a 2013 article, The *Economist* advertised an interestingly strong negative relationship between worker productivity and hours worked.[31]

The article's interpretation of the data, however, were different to mine: they argued that they show that fewer working hours *cause* worker productivity to increase, not the other way around.

If this were true, we'd expect that increases in worker productivity would follow with government-imposed restrictions on working hours or work weeks. Iceland conducted a pilot of a four-day workweek. It involved 2500 participants who reduced their workweek to between 35 and 36 hours. Studies documented many social benefits to this policy: employee self-reported happiness rose significantly, for example. However, no noticeable increases in employee productivity were documented.[32]

This ought to provide evidence that reductions in working hours aren't typically responsible for increases in worker productivity; it's the other way around.

Since worker productivity is the best predictor of working hours, we'd logically expect reductions in the length of the workweek to be strongly associated with long-term economic growth and bear no significant relationship with union power or government regulation.

In 1995, Robert Whaples put out a survey to a large number of economic historians. To the question he asked, 80 percent of the respondents agreed: "The reduction in the length of the workweek in American manufacturing before the Great Depression was primarily due to economic growth and the increased wages it brought." Furthermore, around two-thirds agreed with the proposition that labour unions were not the *primary* cause of the reduction in the work week.[33]

Whaples' research goes further. He examined changes in the workweek in 274 American cities and 118 industries. Controlling for a whole host of variables, he finds that economic growth was the primary driver of the decline in the workweek before the Great Depression. Half of the decline was concentrated during the First World War, when between 1914 and 1919 high war demand pushed real wages up by 18 percent. Reductions in immigration during that period explain a fifth of the decline, as employers couldn't find as many workers willing to work such long hours. Electrification also seems to explain a noticeable role, probably because it raised worker productivity, and hence wages. Labour unions, on the other hand, according to Whaples, could only explain around 14 percent of the decline; strikes and aggressive bargaining only reduced hours to "a small degree."[34]

Similarly, once important variables are controlled for, state and local maximum hour regulations appear to have had only a small influence on work hours. Wages, which grew because of economic growth, appeared to be the strongest predictors of local and regional working hours.

Workplace Deaths

The ILO estimates that every year, 2.3 million people die from work-related accidents and diseases. To put that number into perspective, deaths from armed conflict totalled 167,000 in 2015 and annual deaths from preventable diseases number at 1.5 million. These are two issues society tends to care much about – so why isn't more attention given to workplace deaths? These lost lives are more damaging to the living standards than you might think: The ILO estimates that the global economy loses a stultifying *$3 trillion a year* thanks to workplace deaths.[35]

Economic growth can be a surprisingly good remedy to a lack of workplace safety: as societies become richer, businesses have greater access to technology which improves workplace safety. But why would businesses invest in safer work environments? What's their incentive? Investment undeniably costs businesses money. But so does loosing workers to deaths on the job. The incentive for business to improve worker safety is much stronger than you might think. If workplaces are unsafe, the likelihood they will attract workers is reduced. This means they'll have to increase wages, which is a burden they may not be willing to endure. In fact, in Victorian Britain, coal miners would earn wages as much as 86 percent higher than the national average, due to the danger and unpleasantness of the job.[36] In the United States, the coal industry once had by far the highest number of workplace fatalities, primarily because of frequently exploding machinery. The engineer Henry Boies invented a new type of gunpowder cartridge which resulted in many less injuries and deaths upon explosion. It was quickly adopted by mining companies.[37]

There are many reasons for the substantial decline in workplace deaths in the United States during the 19th and 20th centuries. Technological improvements and labour market competition can explain a fair part. Government regulation is a surprisingly weak explanation. Many cite America's Occupational Safety and Health Administration (OSHA). Established in 1970, it enforces heavy regulations on workplaces to ensure worker safety. After its creation, workplace fatalities indeed dropped considerably, from 38 deaths a day in 1970 to 15 in 2019. However, it is rarely mentioned that workplace deaths were already declining before these regulations were put in place. In the 37 years before OSHA was created, workplace deaths per 100,000 workers more than halved. That trend continued in the time the agency has existed, but it experienced no noticeable acceleration.[38] If regulation has no played no discernible role, could union bargaining have been of any importance? That seems more plausible – labour unions did pressure mining companies into adopting De Boies' new technology. However, it appears that worker's compensation insurance offers a far better incentive to businesses to improve workplace safety than pressures from labour unions. In fact, a study by the Cato Institute notes:[39]

> Insurance premiums that take account of workplace safety encourage firms to establish safe and healthy work environments. As the frequency of claims rises, the price of workers' compensation insurance increases, thereby penalizing firms for poor safety records. Michael Moore of Duke University and W. Kip Viscusi of Harvard University estimate that, without workers' compensation insurance [which are state-run], the number of fatal accidents and diseases would be 48 percent higher in the United States.

Economic Freedom and Early Economic Development

The role of economic freedom was essential in the West's rise to prosperity. Sweden, for example, bears testament to this. A seminal 1994 study by Andreas Bergh argues that Sweden's enrichment occurred thanks to "well-functioning capitalist institutions."[40] This is confirmed by a wider body of literature, which suggests that property rights played an essential role in the development of many Swedish economic sectors. Throughout the 19th century, a host of private commercial and savings banks were established, who granted capital to farmers and entrepreneurs who benefitted from clear legal entitlements.[41] In fact, according to the Historical Index of Economic Liberty, from 1850 to 1900, economic freedom in Sweden rose considerably, by a whole 1.4 points.[42] It is no wonder, therefore, that the greatest improvements in Swedish social indicators preceded the major expansions of the welfare state in the 1930s during the Great Depression. From 1861–1870 to 1921–1930, infant mortality per 1000 births fell from 140 to 60 and the life expectancies of both men and women increased by roughly 40 percent.[43] Furthermore, in 1920, the richest 1 percent of the Swedish population held less share of total national income than most other Western countries, and it had declined noticeably over the previous 20 years – all before large welfare programs were initiated.[44]

Europe's early enthusiasm for free markets undoubtedly explains why it rose to prosperity faster than other continents and empires. Paul Roberts and Karen Araujo note,

> Innovations that catapulted England into the Industrial Revolution did not occur in Spain or the Spanish colonies because the conditions did not foster an entrepreneurial climate. In Spanish America, potential innovators were comfortably ensconced in the government or the church.[45]

There is the argument that Europe enriched itself off the back of imperial and colonial exploitation. This can only be said to be a complete myth. In 1770, all profits from the slave trade, had they been entirely invested in the British economy, would have accounted for only 3 percent of total capital formation at the time. Economic historian Deidre McCloskey wrote in her seminal book, *The Bourgeoisie Deal*,

> [t]he trade in slaves, quite a small part of Britain's or Europe's trade, could not have been the cause of British or European prosperity. As Stanley Engerman and Patrick O'Brien showed… the so-called profits were too small. To attribute great importance to a tiny trade would make every small trade important—we are back to the brass industry as a cause of the modern world.[46]

The favourability of business climates was a good predictor of early economic development. England, for example, is generally seen to have been the first European country to begin to industrialise. England had had a functional patent system from as early as 1624 – while other European countries didn't establish their own until the 1790s.[47] This accounts for why many of the Industrial Revolution's greatest innovations took place in England. Even more curiously, England didn't have a particularly well-educated workforce, either. A survey of 498 applied scientists and engineers born in the 50 years after 1700 found that only 28 percent had been to prestigious Scottish universities or had inhabited the lofty towers of Oxford or Cambridge universities. The vast majority had had no formal university education. They had mostly acquired their knowledge through apprenticeships, pragmatic experience, or informal relationships with those with more knowledge.[48] This should demonstrate that to be innovative, developing economies do not really need especially educated workforces, but good economic frameworks instead.

The greatest gains in economic freedom in the West occurred during the 1800s, according again to the Historical Index of Economic Liberty (Britain also had the freest economy in 1850, for when the earliest data is available).[49] Throughout the 19th and early 20th centuries, taxes and public sector involvement in the economy remained low in the West. From 1870 to 1914, taxes remained below a tenth of national income in France, Sweden, Great Britain, and the United States.[50] In most of West Europe, North America, and Oceania, over roughly the same period of time, government spending stayed at or below 20 percent of GDP. After significant deteriorations in freedom took place across Europe and North America during both wars, it increased throughout the 1950s and 1960s.[51]

CHAPTER 3

Economic Liberalism, the Theory: It's All About Competition

These first two chapters have focused on the importance of economic growth in reducing poverty and raising living standards. In the following chapters, it will be examined how economic liberalism is the best system to stimulate growth.

Economic liberalism – otherwise known as free-market capitalism – is a system of private property rights, where trade and industry are run by private enterprise, with minimal government interference through taxation and regulation. This system is often associated with greed, the exacerbation of poverty, and worker exploitation. Such claims ignore the long intellectual tradition which has defended the basics of market economics. In this chapter, I hope to elucidate the arguments for why economic liberalism is inherently best disposed to increase national income and raise living standards.

As suggested by the chapter title, competition is essential to how the marketplace functions. This was brilliantly articulated in 1776 by economist and moral philosopher Adam Smith in his masterpiece *The Wealth of Nations*: "It is not from the benevolence of the baker, the brewer or the butcher that we expect our dinner, but from the regard to their own self-interest."[1] Profit-seeking businesses lack altruistic motivations: they don't care for the pleasure of their customers on selfless grounds, but rather because they see customer needs and desires as opportunities from which they can derive profit. This gives firms a huge incentive to innovate and invent new products, in order to capitalise on unrealised consumer interests. It also incentivises firms to lower the costs of their goods: suppose that, in a market, the average cost of good *A* is $200. Many consumers are not willing to pay this amount of money for *A*. Entrepreneur *B* recognises this, and thus realises a massive business opportunity. Having set up a business, they sell *A* for $100 instead. This attracts a big consumer audience who are unwilling to buy *A* for $200. They flock to *B*'s business, rewarding him with a vast income.

A free market economy promotes competition. It is true that powerful corporate monopolies can arise – but this is only a result of them outsmarting their competitors in the first place. As economic historian Burton Folsom documents in *The Myth of Robber Barons*, throughout the 19th century, during the period of the Gilded Age, businesses built wealth by introducing services valued by millions of people. John Rockefeller introduced cheap oil and provided the masses with energy; James Vanderbilt cut the price of rail fares by 90 percent and Andrew Carnegie lowered the price of steel by 60 percent.[2] In the modern world, increases in living standards are strongly attributable to entrepreneurs. Take Malcolm McLean, who invented containerised shipping in 1960s, which itself has significantly lowered the cost of global free trade. Take the company Searle, which generated millions of dollars from the invention of contraceptives in 1965. Take Steve Jobs, who revolutionised communication with the invention of the iPhone. If that isn't enough, take BiomTech, who saved the world from a pandemic in November 2020 with the creation of a highly effective vaccine.[3]

There is wider empirical confirmation of the theory that competition increases economic welfare, especially in the product market. A 2006 study of the US food industry found that if market concentration becomes duopolistic (where two main firms control the market), 'consumer surplus' is reduced by three-quarters.[4] A study of Mexico's telecommunications market found that weak competitive forces had meant that consumers were paying an extra $25.8 billion over a four-year period than if competition had been stronger.[5] A study of food markets in the same country concluded that poorer income groups suffer substantially more than richer ones from high market concentration. (Other research from both developed and developing countries has confirmed that low-income consumers suffer much more from high monopoly power than richer consumers[6]) A particularly interesting study of energy markets in developing countries over a 15-year period found that competition raises quality as well as lowering prices.[7] It seems that overall, a lack of competition harms developing countries much more than rich ones. In fact, academics examined a large group of cartels in 20 developing countries over an almost two decade period. The economic damage resulting from higher prices translated into a whole 1 percent of GDP.[8]

Sometimes, faith in competition as a means to increase welfare is seen as naïve, due to the *price inelasticity of demand*: the more consumers value something, the greater the economic power imbalance between buyers and producers, so even if the price of that good remains immensely high, consumers will still be willing to buy them. Pharmaceutical products are frequently given examples of this. If a diabetic is unwilling to pay an exorbitantly high price for, say, insulin, their health will be severely compromised. This gives producers an opportunity to keep those prices immensely high. Cases such as this are commonly seen as examples of 'market failure'. However, proponents of the inelastic demand criticism tend to ignore case studies which would probably contradict their argument: food, for example, is far more essential for everyday life than most pharmaceutical drugs. Yet has this resulted in exorbitantly high prices? No. Most food is comparatively cheap to other goods. Drugs being incredibly expensive, in the United States at least, is explained by mainly two factors: enormous production costs and government regulation. In the United States, the Food and Drug Administration (FDA) approves drugs for when they pass safety standards. Nobody would deny that regulation is necessary to a degree to prevent dangerous drugs from entering the market. However, eventually, regulations can become so intense that their costs outweigh their benefits. The costs include substantially higher drug prices. The estimates of the costs which regulations impose on pharmaceutical firms vary, but a 2003 study of 68 different drugs put the cost at $400 million; another study put the 2007 cost at a staggering $960 million.[9] Higher production costs are simply passed onto consumers in the form of higher prices.

Similarly, there is the argument that profit-driven competition fails to be incentivised to produce the goods and services with the greatest societal benefits. Once again, the pharmaceutical market tends to be the villain of this argument. Companies are often accused of avoiding investment in very important drugs, while profiting off addictive but dangerous and ineffective drugs with massive consumer demand, such as opioids (which have contributed to a deadly addiction crisis in the United States). It cannot be forgotten that excessive regulations – which are significantly more burdensome in the United States than in other countries – tend to reduce the incentives to produce drugs, or simply reduce the flow of new drugs into the market. As one article points out:

> The CEI (Competitive Enterprise Institute) has noted that in recent years thousands of patients have died because the FDA has delayed the arrival of new drugs and devices, including interleukin-2, taxotere, vasoseal, ancrod, glucophage, navelbine, lamictal, ethyol, photofrin, rilutek, citicoline, panorex, femara, prostar, omnicath, and transform. Prior to FDA approval, most of these drugs and devices had already been available in other countries for a year or longer.[10]

Besides, the claim that the pharmaceutical industry lacks interest in developing new and needed drugs is simply untrue: one estimate found that the industry has invested $91.9 billion into developing oncology drugs, for example. Estimates show that 34 percent of pharma's assets in development are for cancer drugs.[11]

Regardless of the inequality in power, competition, if unhampered by regulation and deliberate monopoly privileges, will almost certainly improve quality and lower costs for all kinds of goods and services.

Some argue that lowering costs to sell products to low-income consumers is not a profitable business strategy, so competitive markets have no incentive to increase the welfare of the poorest. Various case studies suggest that this is false, many of which will be referred to again in the coming chapters: Monsanto created the Combi-Pack, a package of basic seeds and fertilisers, which were sold at low cost to poor farmers in Africa; Safaricom, a Kenyan company, launched a mobile phone money transfer service aimed at low-income consumers, and banks are racing to replicate it; Celtel took advantage of the world's most underdeveloped telephone market, the Democratic Republic of the Congo. They built telephone lines and offered cellular services at just a few dollars; Africa's fastest developing infrastructural commodity, telecoms, derives much of its investment from the private sector; Muhammad Yunus set up a microcredit scheme in Bangladesh, which gave low-interest loans to small businesses in predominantly rural areas; privately run schools play an integral role in India's education system; the companies Pfizer and Prevnar are the two biggest producers of pneumococcal vaccines, which reached sales of $7.5 in 2019, mostly in poor countries. They're facing competition, however, from Merck & Co, who are developing vaccines against more aggressive strains of pneumococcus.[12]

Contrary to popular belief, developing countries contain enormous attractive consumer markets. In 2015, total private consumption in Africa was $1.4 trillion, and is one of the fastest growing in the world.[13] Africa currently offers a huge untapped potential which companies should be keen to invest in – and access to those markets by foreign investors and businesses is impeded by the economic policies most African governments maintain.

In a competitive market comes innovation, which is essential to long run economic growth and increasing overall living standards. The economist Arthur Schumpeter said famously, "[T]he capitalist achievement does not typically consist in providing more silk stockings for queens but in bringing them within reach of factory girls."[14] Schumpeter's theory is that to generate income, entrepreneurs are forced to invent – and it is the rest of society who predominantly benefits. While he never produced substantive empirical research on these matters, other researchers have tried to subject his theories to statistical analysis. A 2004 paper by William Nordhaus tried to do just this. Using statistical models consistent with the Schumpeterian profits model, they conclude that:

> [O]nly a minuscule fraction of the social returns from technological advances over the 1948-2001 period was captured by producers, indicating that most of the benefits of technological change are passed on to consumers rather than captured by producers.[15]

The paper finds that only 2.2 percent of the total present value of social returns to innovation are captured by innovators themselves – that leaves the remaining 97.8 percent to the rest of society. The value markets create, it seems, is widely shared. Furthermore, evidence suggests that regulations and taxation tend to present obstacles to innovation. A study by economist Ufuk Akcigit found that taxation reduces the total quantity of innovation in any given time and location. Corporation tax can significantly increase burdens on companies trying to invest in R&D and innovate.[16]

Competition can easily be shown to benefit consumers in the product market. Pundits doubt that it can do the same for workers in the labour market. The relationship between a market competitiveness and societal benefits is more complex in the labour market than in the consumer market. In the labour market, competition is not the primary driver of wage growth. The raising of worker productivity does, and competition between businesses for workers ensures that wages equal marginal labour productivity.

Capitalists invest in physical capital to increase the productivity of workers. This includes purchasing better machinery and improving the technological situation of the business. The Austrian economist Ludwig von Mises argued in 1962 that the United States enjoyed the world's highest standard of living because the total amount of capital invested per worker was higher than in most countries.[17]

The phenomenon of capital accumulation causes wages to rise. In fact, in one article, economist Steve Landsburg notes that capital invested per worker strongly correlates with workers' wages. 'Low capital' countries, as we might call them, like India and Nigeria, tend to have significantly lower wages, whereas 'high capital' countries like the United States and Japan, have significantly higher ones.[18]

Further literature has found a strong relationship between capital investment and labour productivity growth. In a free-market environment, the more productive and capital-rich a firm is, the better off its workers tend to be. Larger firms tend to be more capital-rich – and thus, one would one expect them to pay workers higher wages than in small firms. The literature consistently confirms this expectation. As documented in a 1987 study, workers' wages are 13 percent higher in firms with more than 1000 workers, and 8 percent higher in the 500–999 range, than in firms with fewer than 25 workers;[19] a 2018 article by *Jacobin* – a publication not known for its supportiveness of capitalism – reported that firm size strongly correlates with workers' wages. Businesses with four or fewer employees pay less than $1000 per week. But businesses with more than 1000 employees pay around $1700 per week.

On top of that, the article notes, while less than a quarter of businesses with nine employees or fewer offer health insurance, virtually all of businesses with more than 1000 do.[20] This should refute the notion that companies get rich through worker exploitation and suppressing wage growth. This is consistent with evidence from the developing world. As will be noted in Chapter 7, multinational corporations which locate in developing countries tend to pay wages substantially higher than their local competitors, if they are still incredibly low from rich world perspectives.

Similarly, a 2010 study by economists Nicholas Bloom and John Van Reenen contained the following words:

> We... collected information on aspects of work-life balance such as child-care facilities, job flexibility, and self-assessed employee satisfaction. Well-managed firms actually tended to have better facilities for workers along these dimensions.[21]

The growth of worker productivity is significantly affected by a country's regulatory environment. If government regulation and interference with the market process becomes too intense, businesses find it more difficult to make significant capital investments. Ultimately, this reduces the productivity of the business and workers within the business – thereby leading to lower wages. In 1999, economists Robert Hall and Charles Jones found that most of the variation in output per worker between rich and poor countries could be explained by what they called 'social infrastructure' – in simpler language, government policy. The economists argue: "Countries with corrupt government officials, severe impediments to trade, poor contract enforcement, and government interference in production will be unable to achieve levels of output per worker anywhere near the norms of western Europe, northern America, and eastern Asia."[22] The importance of this particular study shouldn't be underestimated. Severe regulatory barriers to business activity – which later chapters will confirm developing countries tend to have – seems to be a strong barrier to worker productivity growth. This strongly vindicates the central message of this book: that economic deregulation is integral to the alleviation of global poverty.

A second reason why worker productivity is affected by regulation is because the average size of firms may be reduced. As established, bigger firms tend to be more productive, and thus pay higher wages. Therefore, regulations with the unintended effects of preventing firms from upsizing would reduce average worker productivity. According to one study, African firms are on average 20 percent smaller than their counterparts in other locations. The researchers who wrote the study proposed a multitude of different reasons for this: poor access to electricity, finance and electricity, and a dysfunctional legal system. However, the role of regulations on firms cannot be understated. The authors of the study note that as African firms grow, the number of regulations they have to deal with rises massively. In fact, in Niger, a firm with 100 employees spends 14 percent more time dealing with government regulations than a firm with 50 employees. Quite understandably, this discourages firms increasing in size – and harms the rest of the economy as a result.[23]

Worker productivity growth is essential to wage growth. However, it is necessary that the conditions exist so that workers' wages equal their productivity. This is having a competitive labour market is important. If the labour market is monopsonist – where there is a highly limited number of buyers of labour – then wages will be suppressed. If the market is competitive, on the other hand, then this won't be a problem and wages will equal productivity.

Thus, there is empirical evidence that labour market competitiveness can affect wages. A classic example is when, in 2018, Amazon raised its minimum to $15 an hour. A study three years later found a 10 percent increase in Amazon advertised hourly wages led to a 2.6 percent increase in wage offers from businesses in the same commuting zones.[24]

Less anecdotally, a 2017 study by economist José Azar tried to analyse the impacts of market concentration on wages. A market being controlled by a handful of firms would certainly reduce competition; and if the competition model of the labour market is plausible, we'd expect market concentration to have a negative impact on wages. And, according to this study, it certainly does:

> We show that going from the 25th percentile to the 75th percentile in concentration is associated with a 17 percent decline in posted wages, suggesting that concentration increases labor market power.[25]

A study from the UK found that the same increase in concentration reduces wages by 1.1 percent. Though not nearly as large as Azar's findings, this still suggests concentration can exert a significant impact on wages.[26]

Another study from the United States found that a slight reduction in labour market concentration since 1976 had meant that in 2015, average earnings were 1 percent higher and the ratio between the poorest and richest workers 6 percent lower than if the market had been as concentrated as in 1976.[27]

Competition is key to overall increased market efficiency, firm productivity, and thus long-run economic growth, which is what the developing world needs. A 1990 study by Jonathon Haskel, using data from the U.K from between 1980 and 1986, finds that high levels of market concentration significantly reduce firm productivity.[28] This implies that when the market is competitive, businesses have incentives to economise on resources and behave as competently as possible, because in a situation of high market concentration there are much fewer firms competing with one another, so those incentives are greatly compromised.

In 2010, Thomas Holmes and James Schmitz published a meta-analysis of studies on many different industries. Specifically, changes in the competitiveness of the economic environment were studied. Practically all the literature they reviewed demonstrated a strong correlation between increased competition and increased productivity.[29]

In fact, both studies mentioned came from a large study by the British government's Competition and Markets Authorities, which revealed an endless list of studies on this matter. In their own words:

> The evidence suggests that competition drives productivity in three main ways. First, within firms, competition acts as a disciplining device, placing pressure on the managers of firms to become more efficient. Secondly, competition ensures that more productive firms increase their market share at the expense of the less productive. These low productivity firms may then exit the market, to be replaced by higher productivity firms. Thirdly, and perhaps most importantly, competition drives firms to innovate, coming up with new products and processes which can lead to step-changes in efficiency.[30]

Productivity growth is very much needed for overall economic growth to occur. A 2006 study by Peter Warr examined data from Thailand and Indonesia over the period 1981 and 2002 and concluded that productivity in the agricultural sector was the main driver of economic growth in the two countries.[31]

How can governments across the world, but especially in developing nations, boost competition? As we shall see later on, governments of developing countries make setting up businesses and participating in a market incredibly difficult, due to excessive red tape – a study, using World Bank data on 118 countries, found that the tax administrative burden significantly reduces the entry of new firms into the market.[32] Furthermore, a study of European firms found that entry regulations greatly restrict the number of new businesses which enter the market.[33] The pro-competition effects of economic deregulation would have enormous implications for economic growth in the developing world. A study led by economist Simeon Djankov split countries up into four quartiles in terms of business freedom. The researchers found that ascending from the bottom to the top quartile could boost growth by an astounding 2.3 percentage points a year![34]

Since regulations tend to prevent many smaller businesses from participating in the economy, it is understandable that bigger corporations tend to be advocates of increased regulation, to protect themselves from competition. A much-cited study by William and Nicole Crain found that, in the United States, the cost of regulatory burden for small businesses is 36 percent higher than for large ones.[35] Amazon, famously, supports passing legislation mandating a 15/hour minimum wage, knowing that smaller retail companies will suffer significant burdens, to Amazon's advantage.[36] In fact, research by James Bessen analysed the various factors behind the rise in corporate profits since the 1980s. Obvious ones, like R&D spending and capital investment, accounted for most of the rise. However, the study also found that regulations passed thanks to lobbying pressures account for a worrying portion of the increase as well. The role this factor has played has become especially pronounced since 2000.[37]

Even in developed economies, where business freedom is (relatively) high, entry level deregulation has been shown to boost firm entry into the market, which has translated into competitive benefits. A study of Italian retail firms found that greater entry barriers benefit inefficient incumbent businesses by increasing their profits, a result of lower productivity and higher consumer prices. Deregulation is found to positively affect investment and employment.[38] Furthermore, a study from Portugal found that deregulation had had a modest, albeit limited, effect on firm entry.[39] Even more interestingly, a study found that the deregulation the European service sector would boost the value-added growth rate of the industry by 1 percent point annually.[40]

This does not mean that regulation does not have a role to play in improving competition. Anti-trust laws can reduce market concentration as they did in 20th century America. On top of that, more effective price transparency regulations can incentive companies to lower costs. A 2003 study by the OECD found that such policies were radically successful in lowering various commodity prices in a host of developing countries.[41]

Though rarely mentioned, another factor which may well be inhibiting productivity growth in less developed economies is the popularity of family-owned businesses. Some 85 percent of large firms in Southeast Asia are family-owned, 75 percent in Latin America, 67 percent in India and 65 percent in the Middle East.[42] Evidence shows that family firms are less efficient than typical firms.[43] This is probably because people are allocated to managerial positions in those firms based on their family relations, instead of their actual competency. Granddad might make you a senior executive of his company, even if he knows you won't do a particularly good job compared to someone else the owner isn't related to. But he wants to give a good job and help support you – it's called being a part of a family. However, a widespread misallocation of talent could cause largescale disruptions to economic efficiency and productivity.

Liberalising trade, on the other hand, would also be a very good way to spur competition and hence boost productivity growth. For example, in the 1970s and 1980s, Chile underwent substantial trade liberalisation reforms. Research has attributed large increases in Chilean firm productivity since then to those reforms.[44] Similarly, evidence from a large body of Indian industries found that trade liberalisation did much to inject competition into all industries, but especially concentrated ones, with the effect of noticeably reducing price–cost margins.[45]

How, then, do firms behave in the absence of competitive pressures? There are many different situations where this could be the case. Of course, they may lobby for regulations protecting them from such. But natural monopolies are possible too. For example, De Beers was a South African mining company which operated on much of the world's diamond reserves, which were mostly in Africa at the time. Enjoying this monopoly position, they were able to keep the price of diamonds high for a long time (however, eventually diamond mining began elsewhere, and De Beers' market share collapsed).[46]

State policies often contribute to the existence of unproductive monopolies. For example, these include subsidies to businesses. Research has concluded that although subsidies may boost economic productivity in the short-run, in the long-run, they may inhibit it, because after a while the subsidised businesses start to diminish in terms of productivity. Since they're protected from competition by the subsidies, they do not go out of business. This presents obstacles to more productive businesses entering the market, who are unable to crowd out the less productive businesses.[47] An especially popular economic policy in the developing world is 'industrial policy', where governments deliberately try to promote certain business sectors by protecting them from competition with an array of tariffs, subsidies, and special tax breaks. Scholars who have reviewed the literature on this matter have found no evidence that this policy works to benefit the economy, for three possible reasons: firstly, the policy is predicated on the idea that a country's failure to experience industrial growth is a result of 'market failure', when in fact it is due to already-existing government involvement in the economy, so additional intervention may make matters worse; secondly, the politically powerful tend to capture the benefits of subsidies and distortive tax breaks, as has infamously been the case in Tunisia; and thirdly, industrial policy fails to distinguish between successful and unsuccessful firms within specific sectors of the economy, instead aiming distortive policies at the whole sectors themselves. This gives unproductive firms competitive advantages.[48]

The most monopolistic kind of businesses tend to be state-owned. Since there is only one government, there is only one government-run firm in a particular industry. Often, the private sector is prohibited from competing alongside the state. These kinds of companies tend to be particularly inefficient. Take, for example, Nigeria's state-run steel industry, which has not produced a single bar of steel. Or take the DRC's state-run electrical company: while the company possesses an enormous budget, only 10 percent of the country's population has access to electricity. Or take South Africa's publicly owned electricity sector, Eskom, which runs 90 percent of South Africa's electrical market, and which is found to have a strongly negative effect on economic growth, due to the frequency of power cuts. Or take Mongolia's state-run companies, which eat up large portions of government expenditure and crowd out investment into education and health.[49]

The incompetence of the state-run firms demonstrated above reflects deeper issues which tend to plague them, namely problems of efficiency. In the absence of competitive pressures, there is little incentive for bureaucracies to meet deadlines, economise on resources, and improve standards. Typically, if a publicly owned company's project is failing, the government will simply pour more money into it the next year. Extreme efficiency usually means an incredibly poor service, as described above.

A second, but rarely mentioned issue, is environmental degradation. State-run companies are much less responsive to market price signals than private firms are, so their resource use is superfluous and wasteful. This is why the communist East Germany was so much more polluted than the free-market West; research by the World Bank confirmed that exorbitant air pollution inhabitants of the Soviet Union suffered could be mostly attributed to heavily subsidised energy markets by central planners.[50] A study from Eastern Europe found that private energy firms emit as much as 55 percent less sulphur dioxide than their state-sector counterparts.[51] Evidence from China confirms the argument that private companies are less environmentally impactful than public ones.[52] Similarly, Mexico's state-run energy companies are known for being

The Need for Freedom

substantially more polluting than presumably their private sector counterparts.[53] This is not to say that the private sector is never responsible for environmental wrongs – it merely points out that incentivising efficiency via the profit system is a good way to reduce waste and the overuse of resources. In fact, a study by the thinktank Carbon Brief found that reduced electricity use by industries explains a whole fifth of the total reduction in US carbon emissions since 2005.[54] Pollution is a big issue in many developing countries. While regulation will undoubtedly play a role in reducing it, policymakers must emphasise the natural resource efficiency of the market.

Indebtedness also tends to plague state-owned companies, compared to private ones: a study from China found that state-run firms are much more likely to be in debt and have weaker returns on assets than their private sector counterparts.[55] If these companies can be propped up by tax-funded subsidies, they're more likely to be financially reckless and unable to pay back their loans. The message is clear: state-run companies are strong evidence that competition is necessary for putting firms in shape and improving the use of resources of capital.

This does not mean that monopolistic firms are always bad – corporations only build wealth because they make products which attract consumers in the first place; in fact, emerging economies benefit significantly from the intervention of big multinational corporations. However, if a corporation remains monopolistic for too long, without significant competitive threats being made against it, its entrepreneurial energy can age and disappear. The ambitions for growth and innovation can be replaced with the desire for protection and passive self-maintenance; corporations divert money from R&D spending to lobbying for increasing regulation on their competitors and economic protection. This inevitably comes at the expense of consumers. Why, for example, is US sugar around 40 percent higher the global average price? Simple. Uncle Sam has treated the sugar industry with high tariffs on imports of sugar, thus isolating them from competition. This has certainly helped protect jobs in sugar industry.[56] But at what costs? One study found that this has caused Americans to pay a total extra $1.4 billion for sugar.[57] Moreover, a 2006 Department of Commerce study found that, for every job in the sugar industry, which is protected, three are lost in confectionary manufacturing industries.[58] And a US Trade Commission study found that the abolition of these tariffs would increase total consumer welfare by $276 million.[59] Similar policies exist in Kenya to protect its own sugar industry and maize markets. Of course, they have been greatly detrimental to consumer welfare – research suggests that government intervention directly inflates the price of maize by 20 percent. In fact, research also finds that the complete removal of trade barriers could cause sugar prices to drop by 28 percent and lift 1.2 percent of the population out of poverty. Similar reforms to the maize industry could lift 1.8 percent of the population out of poverty.[60]

If you could sum up why economic liberalism works in one word, you'd say this: competition.

CHAPTER 4

Economic Liberalism is What the Developing World Needs

The previous chapter analysed why economic liberalism works to lift living standards. This chapter will argue that developing countries lack economic liberalism and will review the enormous body of empirical research which shows that maintaining a relatively free market is the best way to stimulate long-lasting economic growth.

Many attribute modern-day global poverty to the long-term impacts of colonial exploitation. There is certainly a degree of truth to this: a study by Nathan Nunn of Harvard University obtained records on the number of slaves exported from African countries. In his words, he uncovered "a robust negative relationship between the number of slaves exported from a country and current economic performance."[1] Colonialism, we must not forget, was itself a suppression of economic freedom and property rights. Imperialists often sought to heavily centralise and regulate their colonies' economic systems: the Belgians forced Rwandan coffee farmers to sell to a single market; the Spanish Empire placed their South American colonies under burdensome tariffs and draconian regulations of even the smallest businesses. In fact, the colonies which received the most economic freedom from their imperial overlords have generally prospered the most after independence – Botswana being the largest example, to be discussed later.[2]

On top of that, there is reasonably strong evidence that nations can be kept poor by geographical constraints. In fact,

The Need for Freedom

Jeffrey Sachs and Andrew Warner found in a 1997 study that landlocked-ness can reduce annual economic growth by 0.3 percentage points, due to how much it impedes trade.[3]

The long-run economic impacts of colonialism and geographical factors have been amplified by the economic policies implemented (or rather, continued) after independence from colonial powers was obtained. In a later chapter, we will examine the African exceptions to this, which are typically the ones who prospered after independence.

A variety of thinktanks have devoted lots of attention to major differences in economic policy between developed and non-developed economies. These thinktanks include: the World Bank, the Fraser Institute, the Legatum Institute, and the World Economic Forum (WEF). The research of each shall be reviewed in this chapter.

Most of these thinktanks' research convey a universal message: economic liberalism is a uniqueness of the developed West; property rights, entrepreneurial freedom, and monetary soundness are privileges of richer countries. The poor, on the other hand, are stuck with bureaucrats, kleptocrats, incompetent public enterprises, wasteful international aid programs, and governments which display no respect for basic property rights, and economic and civil liberties.

Let's begin with the World Bank. Every year, they release the Ease of Doing Business Index.[4] It measures a variety of factors, namely regulatory obstacles to doing business: how long it takes to start a business, how well legal institutions enforce contracts, ease with which construction permits can be obtained, how easy it is to register property, how permitted businesses are to trade across borders, how easy it is to access electricity, and the efficiency and burdensomeness of the tax system. Richer countries perform notably better on the index than do poorer countries. In 2020, the top ten performers on the index were: New Zealand, Singapore, Hong Kong, Denmark, South Korea, United States, Georgia, United Kingdom, Norway, and Sweden. The bottom ten performers, on the other hand, were:

Timor-Leste, Chad, The Democratic Republic of the Congo (DRC), Central African Republic, South Sudan, Libya, Yemen, Venezuela, and Eritrea.

There are noticeable differences in living standards and economic performance between the top and bottom ten performers – Hong Kong, Singapore and South Korea built themselves up from post-war poverty to being some of the richest countries in the world, and Georgia is doing the same after decades of impoverishment under communist rule.

The worst ten performers, however, are in very different economic situations. Many, such as Libya, South Sudan and the DRC are conflict-ridden. All ten of these countries, many would agree, have incredibly low living standards

The World Bank's research finds that economic informality – commonly known as the size of the 'black market' – is strongly associated with regulatory obstacles to doing business. Economic informality is an especially big problem in poorer countries, with a shocking 86 percent of Africa's workforce are employed in the informal sector.[5] The most recent Ease of Doing Business report finds that labour market rigidity strongly predicts employment in black market industries.[6] This is corroborated by larger pieces of literature: a study of 75 countries found that higher regulatory burdens, especially on product and labour markets, allow black markets to grow, alongside reducing overall economic growth.[7] Market *liberalisation* has frequently been the key to stopping widespread illegal market activity. For example, the provincial government of Quebec used to impose very high taxes on tobacco sales. This only led to an enormous illegal market for cigarettes. The tax burden on sales was reduced by 80 percent in 1994, followed by a surge in legal sales of tobacco.[8]

Further World Bank data suggest that economic and financial liberalisation would help promote investment into poorer countries. According to one study, after one or two regulatory reforms on the Ease of Doing Business Index are implemented, developing countries grow at up to 0.4 percent faster than without those reforms, and investment in firms accelerates by 0.6 percent.[9]

Next, meet the Fraser Institute, a thinktank located in Vancouver, Canada. Every year, they release the Index of Economic Freedom. Aside from just business freedom, a host of other variables are examined: how strongly property rights and contracts are enforced, monetary soundness, openness to trade, and size of government. Fraser has been producing the economic freedom rankings since 1970.[10]

The index is split up into four quartiles, from most to least free. Fraser's research finds a strong association between economic freedom and living standards. As of 2020, Per capita income in the highest quartile is $44,198, as opposed to $5754 in the bottom. Life expectancy is 80.29 years in the top, versus 65.62 years in the bottom. The percentage of the population below an income of $5.50 a day is 9.84 percent in the top, versus 72.68 percent in the bottom. The incomes of the poorest 10 percent of the population are $12,293, versus $1558.[11] Other social variables, such as gender equality and infant mortality, are found to have statistically significant associations with economic freedom. In fact, economically freer societies are even found to have lower levels of income inequality. Fraser research from earlier years even discovered that economic freedom moderately positively correlates with tolerance towards homosexuals.[12]

Some object that this index's correlation with living standards cannot be used because it is convoluted by other variables. For example, economically freer societies also happen to have greater democratic freedoms. Perhaps factors such as these in fact drive up living standards, and they just happen to correlate with Fraser's economic freedom index. Various responses can be made to this objection. Many scholars argue that the correlation between economic and political liberty is not coincidental; Milton Friedman postulated that the two are inextricably linked; without mechanisms which can hold governments to account, they will likely begin to centralise the economy and encroach on private property rights.[13]

Of course, democracy can only ever affect growth because of the policies it facilitates the implementations of. An examination of developing countries between 1975 and 1990 found that democratisation to an extent supports economic liberalisation measures.[14] Some research has found that, specifically, democracy strongly contributes to increased protections on property rights, even after controlling for important variables.[15] Furthermore, in a 2007 study, John Dawson wrote:

> Milton Friedman's conjectures on the relation between political and economic freedom are correct… promoting economic freedom is an effective policy toward facilitating growth and other types of freedom.[16]

Some research finds that democracy is only found to benefit economic growth because it tends to lead to greater political stability, lower corruption and overall, more economic freedom, as a meta-analysis of 84 studies confirmed.[17]

On the other hand, we could say that liberalisation *causes* democratisation, or at least allows the economic benefits of democracy to operate, namely by reducing corruption. This is exactly what researchers from Universities in Australia and New Zealand demonstrated: regardless of the political environment, economic freedom can successfully mitigate the effects of corruption, although democratisation significantly helps. On the other hand, corruption will in fact worsen in situations of low economic freedom which nevertheless enjoy the existence of democracy.[18]

On to the Legatum Institute. In 2019 they released the Global Index of Economic Openness (GIEO). In their words, the index aims "to rank 157 countries' openness to commerce, assessing the environment that enables or hinders their ability to trade both domestically and internationally." The index has four pillars: Market Access and Infrastructure, Investment Environment, Enterprise Conditions, and Governance. Within them, sub-pillars include 'import tariff barriers', 'property rights', 'contract enforcement', 'burden of regulation', 'labour market flexibility', and 'rule of law'. The Institute created a measure for what it describes as a country's 'productive capacity'. It attempts to remove two distorting effects of a country's GDP, which can misrepresent a country's productivity: resource rents and demographics. It does this by dividing a country's GDP, without resource rents, by its working age population, to exclude children and the elderly. Dividing the economic openness rankings up into ten deciles, Legatum's researchers find that openness is significantly related to economic productivity. In fact, countries in the most open decile are on average more than eight times more productive than those in the least open one.[19]

Regional and continental disparities in openness are especially noticeable – North America is the highest ranker, while sub-Saharan Africa ranks at the bottom. One also must observe that countries experiencing the greatest rises on GIEO rankings are enjoying the fastest rates of economic growth, such as Georgia, Montenegro, China, and India.

The economist who founded the thinktank, Hernando de Soto, expresses special interest in property rights. In *The Mystery of Capital*, he argues that an absence of property rights in developing countries is one of the greatest explainers of global poverty, because capital cannot be transferred into productive uses. "There are three parts to property rights", he was quoted as saying in the Institute's most recent report, "firstly, it keeps you honest, secondly it identifies you, and thirdly it entitles you. On those three foundations, you build the rest of the edifice."

Finally, let's meet the WEF. They're far from a pro-free-market institution; the thinktank's founder, Klaus Schwab, authored *The Great Reset*, along with Thierry Malleret, which exhorts governments to temper the rising inequalities brought by what the authors see as unfettered market economies, and have been the villains of many right-wing conspiracy theories as a consequence. Nevertheless, WEF's Global Competitiveness Index contains a host of subcomponents. Many of them can be used in our analysis of whether richer countries are on average economically freer than developing ones. These include 'property rights', 'burden of government regulation', 'macroeconomic environment' (which includes budgetary balance, inflationary stability and debt size), 'total tax rates', and 'trade tariffs'. There are others, but we'll stick with these five. I calculated the per capita incomes for the ten best and worst performers on each metric (and the ratios between the incomes of the two groups). The results are displayed below:[20]

Global Competitiveness Index Subtopic	Per Capita Incomes of Top Ten Performers, 2017	Per Capita Incomes of Bottom Ten Performers, 2017	Ratio of Incomes of Top Ten to Bottom Ten Performers
Trade Tariffs	$45,047	$11,433	3.94
Property Rights	$66,365	$8579	7.73
Burden of Government Regulation	$58,812	$30,398	1.93
Macroeconomic Environment	$61,294	$9459	6.48
Total Tax Rates	$41,654	$8681	4.8

These data confirm that economically liberal policies significantly raise living standards, while illiberal economies tend to trapped in poverty. They also show that different policies have varied impacts on prosperity. The highest ratio comes under property rights, at 7.73, while the lowest comes under the burden of government regulation, at 1.93. This vindicates Hernando De Soto's belief that property rights are particularly essential to economic development. Nevertheless, even the smallest ratio is still pretty significant; so, the least effective policy associated with economic liberalism, deregulation, can raise living standards by a lot. In fact, a study showed that had US federal regulations remained constant at 1980 levels, today

US GDP would've been 25 percent larger by 2012 (translating into an extra $13,000 in income per person).[21]

Why have poorer countries shown such great hostility to free markets? In the case of Africa at least, directly after independence many governments would associate free market policies with colonial exploitation. In fact, developmental economists Jeffrey Sachs and Andrew Warner have found that the African countries with colonial histories were more likely to pursue protectionist and statist economic policies.[22]

Most economists acknowledge that secure and stable property rights are the bedrock of a functioning market economy. The relationship between property rights, and growth and living standards deserves even more special attention. A particularly fascinating study by economists at UCLA identified 14 main variables which correlate with national prosperity. The two strongest variables were property rights and, interestingly, black market activity. The study optimistically concludes:

> Liberalizations are, on average, followed by dramatic improvement in country income, while substantial reductions in growth typically follow anti-democratic events. We conclude that countries can develop faster by enforcing strong property rights, fostering an independent judiciary, attacking corruption, dismantling burdensome regulation, allowing press freedom, and protecting political rights and civil liberties.[23]

Another famous study of developing countries came to a few major conclusions: firstly, unsurprisingly, countries with less secure protections on property tend to be poorer. And secondly, poor countries which emerge from a certain level of poverty, yet have weak property rights, have persistently lower incomes than the same countries with strong property rights.[24]

For a broader analysis of the literature, a study by the UK Department of International Development found that research strongly indicates a positive correlation between property rights, economic growth, capital investment and productivity growth.[25] To document some of the literature mentioned in the review, a 1995 study noted that a standard-deviation increase in a constructed property rights index can boost economic growth by 1.2 percentage points annually. A study which examined 860 firms in three African countries found that the ones which enjoyed the strongest property rights were more likely to invest in fixed capital (i.e., machinery, material assets and buildings). Finally, the review offered evidence that increased property rights draws out the benefits of financial liberalisation (a concept to be explored later), which reduces poverty and inequality. These benefits are amplified by strengthening of property rights. Moreover, the potential negatives of financial liberalisation are mitigated by the strengthening of property rights, the research finds.

To truly argue that economic freedom raises living standards, a relationship between freedom and long-run *economic growth* – not just income levels observed at one point in time – must be found. There is a rich body of empirical literature which does just that. Many studies are listed below:

- A 2013 meta-analysis of studies by Joshua Hall and Robert Lawson examined 200 articles on economic freedom, all of which used Fraser's index. Two-thirds of the articles examined identified a positive relationship between economic freedom, growth, living standards and overall national wellbeing. Only 4 percent identified a negative relationship.[26]
- In 1995, the aforementioned Jeffrey Sachs and Andrew Warner produced a seminal study. Their research found that there are a few policies which are required to guarantee stable and long-run economic growth: protection of property rights and reasonable openness to free trade. Countries which had adopted these policies to a specified degree were classified as 'qualifying', and those which hadn't were classified as 'non-qualifying'. The results of this study were striking.

In the authors' words "there is not a single country in our sample... which pursued appropriate economic policies during 1970–1989 and yet which had per capita growth of less 1.2 percent per year, and not a single qualifying developing country... which grew at less than 2 percent per year." In fact, two-thirds of the countries examined which did not satisfy the criteria to be sufficiently economically free experienced 'slow growth' over the 19-year-period studied.[27]

- A 2014 study by Cemil Akin and others reviewed 94 countries over the period 2000–2010, utilising Fraser's index as well. In their words, "as a result of the analyses, it was found that there is a statistically significant positive relationship between the level of economic freedom for all income groups and economic growth." This being said, it was found that different subcomponents of economic freedom have considerably varied impacts on growth.[28]

- In 2006, economists Chris Doucouliagos and Mehmet Ulubasoglu controlled for the effects which physical capital can have on economic growth. Analysing 82 countries over the period 1979–1999, the relationship between economic freedom and growth still exists.[29]

- In the same study which confirmed a strong link between economic freedom and political freedom, mentioned earlier, John Dawson wrote: "(i) free-market institutions have a positive effect on growth; (ii) economic freedom affects growth through both a direct effect on total factor productivity and an indirect effect on investment; (iii) political and civil liberties may stimulate investment; (iv) an important interaction exists between freedom and human capital investment."[30]

- Research by the Serbian thinktank Libek reviewed 92 studies on the relationship between economic freedom and growth. Some 86 of them found a positive relationship, and only 1 found a negative one. It is written in the study, "[T]his shows an unusually high level of agreement among economists that economic freedom indeed has a significant positive impact on the level of economic growth. Policy recommendations would, therefore, be to put all efforts to maximise the level of economic freedom in all ways possible in order to utilize to the maximum this potential."[31]

- In 2011, the Research Institute of Industrial Economics found that a 10 percent increase in the 'size of government' (measured in terms of tax take and spending as a share of GDP) results in a 0.5–1 percent decrease in the annual rate of economic growth, which can have substantial long-term cumulative effects on living standards. The study also addresses the fact there are some countries with high tax rates which have nevertheless experienced strong economic growth. It proposes two possible reasons for this: firstly, these specific countries have high levels of social trust, which minimise the harmful impacts of taxation on growth; secondly (and perhaps more plausibly), these countries have offset the negative effects of high tax rates and levels of spending by maintaining market-oriented policies in other areas.[32]

- In 2009, the Institute for Market Economics reviewed the growth patterns of a large group of OECD countries. The size of government which maximises economic growth, it turns out, is no greater than 25 percent of GDP; and based on a panel data of 81 countries, the optimum level of government consumption is found to be no higher than 10.4 percent. In fact, the study specifies that due to model and data limitations, both these are probably *overestimates*, and the true values are lower.[33]

- A World Bank study examined the relationship between government size and growth. It put countries into quartiles of government size. The lowest indicated government smaller than 25 percent of GDP; the highest indicated greater than 55 percent. Over the period 1995–2010, on a global scale, the lowest quartile experienced a median 2.8 percent annual growth, while the highest experienced just 2.1 percent While this difference may not seem like a lot, it can produce marked differences in prosperity in the long run. Interestingly, the relationship was far more pronounced within Europe. The lowest quartile enjoyed a median growth rate of 6 percent per annum, with just over 2 percent at the top.[34]

- An earlier World Bank study from 2011 observed the economic performance of over 100 countries over the period 1975–2007. It concluded that: "a one unit change in the initial level of economic freedom between two countries (on a scale of 1 to 10) is associated with an almost 1 percentage point differential in their average long-run economic growth rates. In the case of civil and political liberties, the long-term effect is also positive and significant with a differential of 0.3 percentage point." The study also emphasises that the expansion of government power to fulfil 'so-called economic, social, and cultural rights' may, counterintuitively, make people poorer in the long run, because it reduces economic growth.[35]

- A 2020 study by researchers Jamie Pavlik and Vincent Geloso found that countries which had greater levels of economic freedom at the time enjoyed stronger economic recoveries from the Spanish Flu pandemic of 1918–1920. This should be especially relevant to policymakers as I write, as the world emerges from the Covid-19 pandemic, having suffered extensive economic damage.[36]

- In 1997, economist Arthur Goldsmith applied 3 newly developed measures of economic freedom to developing

economies. He found that the ones which score higher on all metrics experience stronger economic growth and perform better on human development indexes.[37]
- A survey of the empirical literature by economist Niclas Berggren finds that overall, evidence is strong for the following: larger public sectors reduce economic growth; free markets are highly conducive to economic growth; robust judicial institutions protect private property rights, and developing countries mostly lack them; monetary recklessness causes inflation, which depresses growth; increasing economic freedom is a good way to reduce income inequality.[38]
- A study of economic liberalisation in Pakistan over the period 1995-2010 concluded that the growth which takes place in economically free systems is strongly 'pro-poor' – meaning those on lower incomes gain comparatively more than the rich. According to the study, economic freedom is strongly associated with reductions in poverty and income inequality.[39]

There is even evidence that greater economic freedom contributes not only to greater income growth, but also higher *income mobility*. This comes mainly from two studies. Firstly, a study by Vincent Geloso (who was mentioned just earlier) and James Dean examined Canadian provinces over a 36-year period and found a positive association between income mobility, especially for people initially from the lowest income deciles, and subnational economic freedom.[40] Secondly, a cross country analysis by Christopher Boudreaux concluded that 'secure property rights and less corruption' are positively associated with higher levels of income mobility.[41] Poorer developing countries, unsurprisingly, suffer from lower level of income mobility. According to the literature, improving economic freedom may be necessary for doing so.

In all the studies I've mentioned, reverse causality could be an issue – perhaps growth, prosperity, and higher income mobility cause more economic freedom in the first place, not the other way around? This was the subject of a study which having analysed various subcomponents of economic freedom, and their relationship with economic growth. It concluded:

> [T]he tests suggest the average level of freedom in a nation, as well as many of the specific underlying components of freedom, precedes growth.[42]

The study noted a caveat, however, that not all elements of economic freedom are seen to precede, and thus possibly cause, economic growth – 'government intervention' being one. Furthermore, the causal directions of economic freedom and economic growth were tested in Bangladesh. Analysing the country over a 20-year period, researchers concluded that increases in economic freedom had clearly preceded accelerations in economic growth.[43] Nevertheless, as is obvious, there is a wide body of literature which speaks positively of the impacts of economic freedom on growth and development. In the next chapter, we will conduct a dissection of economic freedom and do a deeper analysis of its policies.

Eben Macdonald

CHAPTER 5

The Specific Policies of Economic Liberalism

Implementing economic liberalism requires a package of different policies, in the same way implementing socialism requires a combination of radical tax increases, increases in regulation, nationalisations, and hikes in government spending. This chapter will review the main policies which will be required of developing countries to implement the basics of liberalism, and the empirical effects associated with those policies. The policies which this chapter will review are trade liberalisation, privatisation, corporate tax cuts, and labour market deregulation.

Trade liberalisation: through liberalising trade, developing countries will be at a great advantage: they tend to export, not import. Richer countries tend to import cheap products from emerging economies. However, trade liberalisation will almost certainly entail importing goods. Developing countries are largely hostile to this and tend to have much higher tariffs on imports than rich countries do. The average unweighted tariff rate in high-income countries is 2 percent, 4.3 percent in middle-income countries and 9.8 percent in low-income countries. Furthermore, trade takes longer to happen in poorer countries, being as many as 39 days, as in Africa.[1] Tariffs are generally defended on the grounds that domestic industries ought to be protected, and cheaper foreign products could bring competition into domestic markets. The issue with this argument is that it fails to recognise the wider adverse consequences tariffs have on other industries and individuals because of higher prices. The Legatum Institute observes: "Tariffs can make intermediate products less competitive and cost-efficient, raising prices for local consumers. This has been the case in the US, where steel tariffs have made cars more expensive."[2] Recall the case of US sugar tariffs: for every job created in the sugar industry thanks to tariffs, three jobs are destroyed in other industries which are affected by higher sugar prices.

Thus, a 2020 study from U.C Berkeley analysed 151 countries over the period 1963–2014, and concluded:

> Tariff increases are associated with persistent, economically and statistically significant, declines in domestic output and productivity, as well as higher unemployment and inequality, real exchange rate appreciation and insignificant changes to the trade balance. Output and productivity impacts are magnified when tariffs rise during expansions and when they are imposed by more advanced or smaller (as opposed to developing or larger) economies.[3]

It is true that some research has found that trade liberalisation may at times increase inequality. However, it has found at the same time all income tiers are benefitted and overall national welfare improves.

In August 2017, the International Food Policy Research Institute warned that the United States' trade war with China, endorsed by President Donald Trump, would not only hurt emerging countries but under no circumstance could bring any discernible benefits to the US economy. "We conclude," the authors damningly wrote, "that there is no scenario in which the US government augments its domestic welfare or gross domestic product."[4]

Trump's jingoistic 'America First' protectionism was destined to harm the US economy.

The benefits of trade liberalisation are emphasised in basic economic theory: suppose the world's greatest brain surgeon is also the world's fastest typewriter. Should he hire a secretary? Most economists would say 'yes'. If he allocates his typewriting to somebody else, he can specialise at what he is particularly good at, brain surgery. The same principle applies to international free trade: suppose country X has an excess of cars, and country Y has an excess of beer. It is logical for them to exchange products. It may cost jobs in X's car industry or Y's beer industry, but the point is that both countries are better off as a result. This kind of exchange, free trade, is essential to economic growth. The basic rationale for free trade includes lower prices and higher firm productivity, both of which contribute strongly to economic growth.[5]

The World Bank analysed a group of countries over the period 1950–1998. Their findings were that those which liberalised trade grew with an extra 1.5 percentage points of growth than before liberalisation. Investment also rose by 1.5–2 percentage points.[6] Furthermore, the countries which the World Bank designates as 'the new globalisers' together saw substantial reductions in poverty throughout the 1990s, totalling 120 million.[7] According to the International Food Policy Research Institute, the Central American Free Trade Agreement (CAFTA) lowered poverty in Honduras by 11 percent relative to what it would have been in 2020 in the absence of the agreement.[8] In 2012, researchers analysed 108 countries – 87 of which were emerging economies – over the period 1971–2005. Their conclusions were that a one unit increase in the 'rate of trade growth' can increase the per capita income growth rate by 1.16 percentage points over five years.[9]

There have been queries about the causal direction of trade benefits. Some objections hold that countries are only able to trade freely because of appropriate geographical conditions. Other objections hold that countries with higher incomes are only able to do more trade in the first place – incomes increase the amount of trade which occurs, not the other way around.

Also, countries which adopt free trade are likely to adopt other free-market policies, such as lower tax rates, smaller regulatory burdens, and less government spending, all of which affect growth patterns. A study took all other these considerations into account and controlled for variables accordingly. Even so, it still found that trade exerts a positive and statistically significant impact on economic growth.[10]

Trade liberalisation has historically been associated with huge consumer benefits. In the 1840s, Britain repealed the Corn Laws, which had maintained tariffs on corn imports to protect domestic landowners, but with the consequence of keeping food prices high. Within a few years after the tariffs had been repealed, the average Brit was paying a quarter less for bread than had the repeals never happened, and income inequality had declined.[11] More contemporarily, it is estimated that tariff reductions at the Uruguay Round saved European consumers €60 billion in spending.[12] These reductions in costs tend to benefit the poor the most. Because poor consumers spend disproportionately on goods affected by trade policy, a study by the University of California found that erecting large trade barriers can cost the poorest 10 percent of the population as much as 63 percent of their purchasing power! The same study found that a 1 percentage point increase in trade openness is associated with a 0.2–0.6-point reduction in the Gini coefficient, a measure of income inequality.[13]

Liberalisation is also associated with improved firm-level and national productivity. For example, after the Canada–US Free Trade Agreement was signed, the Canadian industries exposed to the greatest tariff cuts on American imports experienced sharp rises in labour productivity.[14] When markets are opened to international competition, firms realise they are fish in much larger waters, and tend to act accordingly. In fact, researchers have also discovered that Argentinian firms responded to enormous reductions in Brazilian tariffs by pumping money into technological development.[15] One of the big reasons why trade liberalisation improves productivity is because it introduces competition into sometimes highly concentrated and monopolistic markets. According to a study using data from Taiwan, trade "strongly increases competition and reduces markup distortions by up to one-half."[16]

Free trade has been found to positively impact gender equality. The Nobel-Prize-winning economist Gary Becker theorised that in a competitive market, businesses would have no incentive to discriminate against job candidates based on characteristics such as race or sex, as such is often costly.[17] Since trade increases business competition on a global scale, it is conceivable that it contributes to a global reduction in the amount of discrimination which happens. Two researchers compared gender wage gaps in competitive versus monopolistic manufacturing firms over a 17-year period. Finding that they shrunk more in the competitive firms, the authors concluded that free trade reduces discrimination against women by increasing market competitiveness.[18] Furthermore, firms which export goods in developing countries tend to employ significantly more women than ones which don't – so increasing trade creates opportunities for women by raising employment and wage levels. This was the case in Mexico, where free trade agreements during the 1990s helped grow sectors such as textiles and clothing, which employed more women, thus raising women's wages and employment.[19] Free trade also reduces the likelihood women will inhabit informal sector jobs, which tend to be lower paid and more insecure.[20]

Free trade has even been discovered to benefit innovation. For example, researchers analysed the GATT Uruguay Round trade agreements of the 1990s. They found that 7 percent of the increase in global knowledge since then could be attributed to freer trade.[21] Why does trade impact innovation? There are many possible reasons why. Maybe to remain competitive, firms must invest heavily in innovating their way to success; for example, one study found that European firms most exposed to trade with China innovated the most.[22] Another theory is that trade allows the international transfer of technology and information, which

The Need for Freedom

boosts innovation. This is confirmed by a lot of literature from across the academic world.[23] Innovation is vital for economic growth and poverty alleviation. Developing countries can make more of it happen through liberalising trade with other nations.

A typical objection to free trade, found both in rich and poor countries, is that it costs jobs in the domestic economy. Addressing the concern that free trade costs the domestic economy jobs, one study writes:

> These costs are typically short term and end when workers find a job, but the benefits grow as the economy does. Unemployment doesn't last long, especially where workers' pay was not substantial in the original job. Normal labor turnover often exceeds job displacement from trade liberalization. Moreover, studies that examine the impact of trade liberalization on employment in developing countries find there is little decline – and usually an increase – in manufacturing employment in developing countries a year after trade liberalization, for three reasons: Developing countries tend to have comparative advantage in labor-intensive industries, and trade liberalization tends to favor labor. Interindustry shifts occur after trade liberalization, which minimizes the dislocation of factors of production. In many industries normal labor turnover exceeds dislocation from trade liberalization, so downsizing, when necessary, can be accomplished without much forced unemployment.[24]

In fact, some research suggests that trade liberalisation *raises* employment in the long run. One piece of research found "fairly robust and strong evidence for the Ricardian prediction" that trade openness reduces unemployment.[25] Research by Istanbul University analysed 87 countries over a 23-year period, finding that a single point increase in trade openness reduces unemployment by 0.6 percent.[26] This is logical, seeing that prices decline, leaving businesses and consumers with more money to spend elsewhere.

I would introduce a vital caveat about trade, however. Countries must make sure that exports are diversified – meaning they export a variety of different products and goods, instead of one single commodity. If demand for that one product suddenly falls for whatever reason, the exporting country could be in a lot of trouble economically. Unfortunately, less developed economies tend to enjoy less diversification. According to multiple reviews by the IMF, export diversification is associated with greater long-run economic growth and macroeconomic stability.[27]

The poverty-reducing capacities of free trade are acknowledged by economists of many different ideological blends. A study by IZA World of Labor reviewed a large body of work on the matter and concluded that trade liberalisation does alleviate poverty, just so long as it is accompanied by domestic institutions such as good infrastructure, protections on workers' rights, and strong financial development.[28] The message is clear: there are large net positive effects to trade liberalisation. Arguments that it costs jobs and reduces domestic living standards are mainly propaganda. Reducing barriers to trade is one of the most effective ways to increase economic growth and reduce poverty.

Financial liberalisation: Banks are essential parts of financial infrastructure – they provide businesses with vital loans and capital, which contributes to job creation, wage growth, and innovation. In 1993, economists Robert King and Ross Levine published their findings on 80 countries over a 30-year period. A clear and robust relationship between financial development and the rate of income growth, infrastructural development, and overall economic development could be seen.[29] Further research confirms just how important credit and private capital are to raising living standards. For example, a ten-point increase in the private credit to GDP ratio will reduce the poverty rate by 2.5 to 3 percentage points.[30]

There is a wealth of literature highlighting the effectiveness of financial liberalisation in stimulating economic development.

A major theoretical contribution to the argument for financial liberalisation came from Ronald McKinnon and Edward Shaw. In contrast to 'financial repression', in which governments hold interest rates down below their market values, financial liberalisation allows an increase in real interest rates. Contrary to the Keynesian opinion, this will allow an increase in the savings rate, and thus investment. Increasing investment is essential to raising economic growth rates. Therefore, financial liberalisation contributes to poverty reduction.[31] This this theory is borne out by a few case studies. In the years after liberalisation took place in Ghana, interest rates indeed rose. There was indeed an increase in the savings rate, and thus a rise in capital accumulation. And consequently, economic growth accelerated.[32] Other countries, such as Iran and Nigeria, have enjoyed higher growth rates in the years after liberalisation, following higher interest rates and levels of savings.[33] However, *whether this specific theory is sound overall*, there are many studies which have identified a link between financial liberalisation, economic growth, and thus poverty reduction.

For example, a study of India concluded that financial availability had strongly contributed to poverty reduction in rural India through "fostering entrepreneurship and inducing geographic-sectoral migration." The rapid expansion in banking credit may well have been a factor in India's dramatic improvement in living standards since the 1990s. In 1980, banking credit accounted for an average of just 18.7 percent of state domestic product (SDP) across India's 15 states. By 2005, that had already risen to 50.3 percent. The study also found that India's credit-SDP ratio increased considerably after the economic liberalisation episode of 1991: from 1983 to 1991, credit rose from roughly 0.2 to 0.25 percent of SDP; from 1991 to 2005, it rose from 0.25 to 0.5 percent.[34]

A study of financial liberalisation in Thailand was especially optimistic. Not only did banking deregulation spawn a new class of entrepreneurs, but workers benefitted as well, albeit indirectly. More entrepreneurs in the market meant higher labour demand, thus higher wages, and average incomes were found to have increased notably thanks to the reforms.[35] Perhaps it is no coincidence then that during this phase of banking deregulation and further economic liberalisation, poverty fell from 42 percent to 15 percent of the population.[36]

A similar phenomenon was witnessed in the United States. From the 1970s through to the 1990s, states repealed intrastate branching regulations, which prevented banks from competing outside the states they were located in. Tearing up these restrictions drastically increased the competitiveness of the banking sector. A study found that the biggest winners from these regulatory reforms were low-wage workers, for approximately the same reasons witnessed in Thailand.[37]

Meanwhile, more longitudinal studies suggest that the deregulation of financial markets boosts economic growth. In 2005, three economists published a study showing that the liberalisation of equity markets boosts economic growth by 1 percent on average.[38] This is probably because businesses are more able to attract equity capital, a vital component of long-term growth.[39] However, not all the literature is entirely optimistic of financial liberalisation's benefits. Some academics found that although the correlation between financial liberalisation and economic growth is strong – and economic growth is a powerful engine of poverty alleviation – the correlation between liberalisation and poverty reduction was in fact weak. Some of this research has relied on very small sample sizes, however.[40]

Many fear that in the absence of effective regulation, banking practises could become predatory, or the financial sector won't make itself available to the poor. To ensure that capital is available, banking markets must be kept competitive, in the same way product prices are kept low, and wage growth is kept steady. A study from 2006 found that in more competitive and transparent banking sectors, eligibility barriers to the poor to accessing banks are lower.[41] The concern that the increase in interest rates resulting from liberalisation will harm poorer borrowers is far more legitimate. However, a study which was mentioned in Chapter 4 shall be repeated here: the benefits of financial liberalisation are amplified, and the negatives heavily mitigated, when such reforms are accompanied by the strengthening of property rights.

The most widespread concern about banking deregulation is that it results in financial crises. There are crises in particular which are blamed on a lack of financial regulation, namely the 2008 Financial Crisis. However, the subprime mortgage program was heavily subsidised by the federal government via Government Sponsored Entities (GSEs), as they were known.[42] At the same time, banking recklessness has too often been encouraged by the willingness of governments to bail them out in times of crisis. Much evidence confirms this. One study examined 345 European banks over seven years, and found that in the year after bailouts alone, banks increased their riskiness by an average of 23 percent. More worryingly still, other banks which hadn't been bailed out displayed higher levels of riskiness, to stay in competition with the ones which had.[43] Another study of American banks after receiving bailouts during the Financial Crisis found not only did they become riskier, but that these increases in risk were undetected by regulatory authorities, because they occurred mostly in the same asset classes. If bailouts are implemented, they can even reduce the capacity of regulation to improve banking safety.[44]

Overall, the evidence that financial liberalisation in developing economies increases the risk of financial crises occurring is weak. In fact, a study of Southern African countries which liberalised their financial institutions in the 1980s and 1990s found that the risk of financial crises occurring had *actually diminished*.[45] A 2005 study by John Boyd and Gianni De Nicolo reviewed the literature and concluded that the link between financial liberalisation and financial crisis is highly tenuous. True, increases in banking competition can lead to large investments in risky portfolios. meanwhile, there are some theories which suggest that increased levels of competition in the banking sector can in fact *reduce* financial instability.[46] According to another study, interest rate liberalisation reduces the likelihood of financial crises happening, because it tends to strengthen banks' 'capital buffers' – extra capital which banks save in the event of emergencies.[47] The study found that the growth of property prices is the greatest driver of financial crises (which is exacerbated, as we shall see later, by excessive regulations on planning markets. In fact, some scholars have attributed the US housing bubble of 2006 specifically to property price growth driven by supply restrictions thanks to zoning regulations[48]).

Privatisation: As discussed in Chapter 3, when state-owned, industries become highly monopolistic, and hence uncompetitive; and an absence of competition reduces the incentives to improve the quality of goods and services. The inefficiency of state-run companies can put serious burdens on national finances, with terrible macroeconomic consequences. A typical example is Mexico, where subsidies to public companies had to be funded by printing money, causing serious inflation.[49] In 1996, the World Bank reported that in the previous year, subsidies to public companies in Mongolia, a country recently emerging from communism, took up 7.4 percent of the nation's GDP, greater than all social welfare expenditure. In fact, the same year, without any subsidies to public companies, Mongolia's budget deficit would only have been a third of its actual size! Inflation in Mongolia remained stubbornly high, at 50 percent per year.[50]

This is because there is strong evidence, meanwhile, that private ownership reverses the inefficiencies of state ownership. Milton Friedman noted that although private holdings were only 1 percent of the Soviet Union's total farmland, they were responsible for a third of the Union's agricultural output.[51] A study of 27 economies found that higher levels of private ownership of 'the means of production', instead of state ownership, is associated with higher income growth.[52] With economic incentives installed, there are then indeed dramatic increases in efficiency and firm productivity. For example, there were major privatisations of infrastructural amenities in the United Kingdom, with great success. Of these privatisations, the OECD notes:

> [T]he evidence shows that the privatised utilities and infrastructure providers: increased labour productivity, and sometimes total factor productivity, at rates faster than those generally achieved before privatisation; offered real price reductions (except in the water industry, where higher charges were needed to fund significant quality improvements). In the telecommunications and gas industries in particular, prices have fallen at a faster rate than they did before privatisation; achieved sustained improvements in levels of service quality, especially in the telecommunications and water industries; and provided very substantial contributions to public sector finances.

These improvements were very competition driven. British Gas, for example, now faces significant competition in supply markets. By 1997, a decade after privatisation, a quarter of domestic customers in southwest and southeast England had switched to alternative suppliers, and the company's market share had fallen below 30 percent by 1997.[53]

This narrative is corroborated by other studies. Michael Wise and Maria Maher demonstrate in one study that regulatory and liberalising reforms brought to UK gas, water and electrical utilities resulted in astounding rates of productivity growth, of up to 10 percent per year throughout the 1990s.[54]

Literature from other countries demonstrates the benefits of privatisation. A large study from Mexico shows massive increases in firm profitability after privatisation, and that 64 percent of this increase could be attributed to gains in productivity. The social benefits of privatisation were also indicated, namely greater access to services among poorer consumers.[55] Another study analysed 12 major privatisations across the world and concluded that welfare gains, measured by the increase in the real value of sales, took place in all but one of them. Fiscal advantages were also emphasised, as pressures are taken off national finances to subsidise state-run industries. The authors of this study attributed the welfare gains to increases in investment and productivity.[56]

It is clear that private enterprises have incentives to improve service quality which governments lack. In the 1990s, many of Argentina's local water companies were privatised. As many economists and thinkers have noted, deaths from unclean water declined by 8 percent as a result of the policy. In fact, this decline was the most pronounced in the country's poorest areas, where it reached 26 percent.[57]

There's the argument that increases in profitability and efficiency in privatised firms only occur to reductions in workers' wages after privatisation. This is a very bold assumption to make with an insufficient amount of evidence behind it. Although privatisation in Brazil was followed by cuts to workers' wages,[58] in some cases, privatisation can lead to an increase in wages: since state-run firms tend to be overstaffed, reductions in firm employment often result from privatisation. A smaller workforce, combined with increases in productivity, results in higher wages (this does not mean, however, that privatization always leads to increases in unemployment. Such fears, as we shall see, are sometimes exaggerated). In Cote d'Ivoire, employee compensation grew by 6.8 percent every year in firms which were privatised.[59] An analysis of 30,000 privatised firms in the post-communist transition economies found that sales to domestic owners exerted a very slightly negative impact on wages, while sales to foreign owners exerted at times *large and positive* impacts. A study of privatisations specifically in Ukraine found that while sales to domestic buyers can reduce wages, sales to foreign ones has no impact.[60]

Evidence from China, where bureaucracy is often supposed to be more efficient than in other countries, shows that private companies perform better on a variety of metrics than their government-owned counterparts, such as innovativeness, return on assets, and overall profitability. The WEF opines:

> It is evident… that SOEs [state-owned enterprises] are highly over-leveraged and structurally less efficient than their private peers. Stagnating growth throughout China's public sector has led to a shrinkage in its overall asset holdings. SOEs are often criticised for abusing their preferential access to loans, and for lobbying for regulations which drive out competitive private companies. It is widely argued that the SOEs would not survive in an innovation-driven market environment without the perks they currently enjoy.[61]

Privatisation is typically associated with enormous increases in firm productivity and efficiency, which is vital for nurturing economic growth in the developing world. A study from 2000 examined 119 privatised firms, in 29 different countries and from 26 different industries, over the period 1961–1995. "Significant increases in profitability, efficiency, output, and capital expenditures, and significant decreases in leverage following privatization" were documented by the researchers.[62] A separate study by the World Bank notes:

> [P]rivatisation improves firms' financial and operating performance, yields positive fiscal and macroeconomic benefits (proceeds are saved rather than spent, transfers decline, and governments start collecting taxes from privatised firms), and improves overall welfare. The popular view that privatisation always leads to layoffs is unfounded.[63]

The study notes that only firms significantly protected from competition shed large numbers of their workforce; firms exposed to competition, on the other hand, experience barely any decline in employment.

A famous study published in the *Lancet* medical journal purported to show that privatisation had led to an increase in mortality rates in several post-communist Eastern European economies, because privatised firms supposedly cut employment significantly. This view of privatisation in Eastern Europe is empirically baseless. A response study controlled for many variables which the previous one had failed to do for; it examined the employment effects in not just privatised firms, but firms which were never sold off, or ones which were yet to be. It also conducted its analysis over a long, 20-year period and reviewed businesses in the same industries to analyse "apples with apples, rather than apples with oranges." The results were fascinating: privatisation generally results in positive effects on employment among domestic buyers, and when negative, they're statistically insignificant. Among foreign buyers, there are generally large and positive effects, increases of between *10 and 30 percent*. On top of that, the authors noticed privatisation exerted large productivity effects. Firm productivity rose by 10–25 percent following acquisition by foreign buyers.[64] There are indeed documented cases of where job shedding has followed privatization. Though far from being the rule, when they do happen, they can even be beneficial.

Some research has focused on a relationship between privatisation and economic growth. Most interestingly, a sample of 35 developing countries found that privatisation can boost growth by between 0.8 and 1.5 percentage points over a four-year period.[65] Another study came up with less optimistic results, finding that a 1 percent increase in privatisation relative to GDP is associated with on average a 0.45 percent increase in economic growth over two four-year periods by significantly improving national finances.[66] The enormous increases in productivity associated with privatisation are necessary for economic growth in the developing world, as it allows economies to absorb the benefits of globalisation and freer trade by becoming more competitive. In fact, a study of Vietnam showed that, after the country's accession to the World Trade Organisation (WTO), if it had not a single state-owned enterprise (SOE), five years later economic productivity might just have been two-thirds higher.[67]

Corporate tax reductions: taxing large businesses is defended on redistributionist grounds, and they're seen as a good source of government revenue. However, the adverse economic effects of corporation tax are rarely considered.

Many do acknowledge that tax competition is a way in which poorer countries can attract investment and capital. For example, Ireland went from a country mired in agrarian poverty to one of the richest countries in Europe thanks in part to maintaining a very low, 12.5 percent corporate tax rate. A handful of developing countries have been able to spur growth through doing the same – Botswana, Morocco, Chile, Turkey and many post-communist East European states being notable examples.

Higher taxation reduces the incentive for companies to expand and commit to capital investment. The OECD took data from 21 countries and concluded that the corporate tax rate had the most negative effect on real GDP per capita out of all the taxes examined.[68]

Taxation on businesses plausibly reduces growth because it discourages business entry. A World Bank study mentioned in an earlier chapter looked at 118 countries and found that this effect is significant. A study using data from 72 countries over a six-year period came to a similar conclusion.[69] Evidence also indicates that reducing taxes would help increase business entry into the market. A study from Brazil showed that, once registration costs have been repealed, tax reductions do in fact increase business entry.[70]

Corporation tax is found to harm workers' wages. A study by Alison Felix estimated that a 10 percent increase in the corporate tax rate reduces workers' wages by 7 percent (with the wages of high and low skilled workers being equally affected)[71]; Kevin Hassett and Aparna Mathur use panel data for 72 countries over a 22-year period, and control for important variables which affect wages. The authors find that a 1 percent increase in the corporate tax rate is associated with an almost 1 percent decrease in wages.[72] You might complain that both these studies are relevant only to rich countries and cannot be compared to developing ones. However, in the latter study, the authors compared OECD and non-OECD countries, which can be used as a fairly rough proxy for developed and underdeveloped economies. Although the correlation between corporate taxation and wages was much stronger in OECD countries, there was nevertheless a statistically noticeable correlation among the non-OECD economies.[73] The basic economic theory the paper was based on suggests that corporation tax will *inhibit* long-term wage growth in the developing world. The more the capital-labour ratio increases, the more worker productivity, and hence wages, rise. If businesses activity is interfered with by taxation, capital investment becomes more difficult in the long run. In the developing world, workers are highly unproductive. I hope the danger, therefore, of corporate taxation in the emerging global market becomes obvious. Furthermore, a 2007 study of the foreign activity of American multinational corporations – from which many developing economies derive their investment – in 50 countries from 1989 to 2014 found that labour bears between 45 and 75 percent of corporate tax burden is borne by labour.[74]

It is plausible that corporation tax would reduce wages in developing economies by scaring away foreign businesses which pay workers incredibly well by national standards. In the penultimate chapter, we will review the strong empirical evidence that multinational corporations which locate in developing countries pay wages far higher than their national averages. Understandably, it would be a huge mistake of developing nations' governments to prevent such huge benefits for workers from materialising, with taxation. After all, a 2018 study found that multinational's decisions to set up foreign subsidiaries is strongly affected by the tax rates of those countries.[75]

Corporation tax reduces economic growth because it is disincentivises Foreign Direct Investment (FDI). For example, reviewing data from 19 OECD countries found that a 1 percent reduction in the corporate tax rate boost FDI by roughly 2.4 percent.[76] Another analysis demonstrated that the same reduction could produce up to a 5 percent increase in FDI.[77] Developing economies are much more dependent on FDI than their richer peers. Maintaining lower corporate tax rates could attract the foreign investment necessary to provide substantial boosts to job growth, entrepreneurialism, and poverty alleviation.

There are a few countries in particular, mostly located in Eastern Europe, which owe their economic successes in recent years to favourable tax environments for businesses – they will be discussed in the following chapter.

On top of all this, there is some evidence that corporate tax increases prices. A 2020 study by Scott Baker and Constantine Yannelis found that an entire third of the corporate tax rate's burden falls on consumers in the form of higher costs. The researchers also discovered that cheaper products typically purchased by low-income consumers see greater inflation in response to corporate taxation.[78] Seeing that emerging markets tend to be driven more low-income consumers, it is conceivable that corporate taxation contributes a sizeable amount to price inflation.

Cutting corporate taxes is a necessary policy for boosting economic growth and increasing capital investment into developing economies. For example, through exempting manufacturing companies from corporation tax for the first five years of setting up or locating in the country, and after that, giving them a flat rate of 8.75 percent, Morocco enabled its industrial sector to grow 12-fold from 2004 to 2015 and create 78,000 jobs in the automotive sector.[79] A feature of China's Special Economic Zones – regions which have pursued market-oriented policies since the end of communism more than others – was special tax incentives to businesses to make investments and create jobs. Most evidence suggests that these Zones have outpaced less economically liberal regions in growth, job creation, and attracting foreign investment.[80]

A report by the World Bank notes that Special Economic Zones are estimated to have created 30 million jobs in China, raised farmers' incomes by 30 percent, and contributed significantly to industrialisation and economic modernisation.[81]

Labour market deregulation: the more regulated a labour market is, the more difficult it may be to hire workers below a specified minimum wage, or fire workers for certain reasons. These kinds of regulations are justified to protect 'workers' rights'. However, they often have unintended economic consequences, harming groups which the regulations were originally designed to help. If businesses know in advance that firing a worker will be either prohibited or simply made extremely difficult by regulatory authorities, they may not take the risk of hiring that job candidate. This incurs a serious problem – unemployment.[82]

Evidence suggests that onerous labour market regulations contribute to unemployment, and hence poverty. Take one of the most important labour market regulations, the minimum wage. There is strong evidence that the policy of raising the minimum wage reduces employment in high-income countries. A study from the United States concluded: "There is a clear preponderance of negative estimates in the literature… this evidence is stronger for teens and young adults as well as the less-educated."[83] Admittedly, though, the evidence for developing economies is more mixed. A meta-analysis of 61 studies led by economist David Neumark found that in developing countries, minimum wages are more likely to reduce the employment levels of unskilled workers in formal sector jobs, especially when the laws are binding and effectively enforced.[84] At the same time, the evidence is surprisingly mixed that minimum wage increases *reduce* poverty in developing countries. For example, although low-wage workers gained substantially on net from minimum wage increases in Thailand and Mexico, they benefitted significantly less in Colombia, Brazil, and Honduras. In fact, in some cases, poverty has risen as a result of minimum wage increases. In the cases of where minimum wage increases have not led to substantial benefits to the poor, this has mainly been due to reductions in employment among low-income households which have mainly offset wage gains.[85] In fact, studies of Indonesian firms find that minimum wage increases can have detrimental impacts on employment, especially for less-skilled, female workers.[86] In fact, some believe Indonesia's relatively high minimum wage has discouraged foreign investment, exposing another problem associated with rigid labour market regulation. In 2019, The Economist reported:

> A survey of firms with ties to Japan by the Japan External Trade Organisation, a government body, shows that the wages of Indonesian manufacturing workers are 45 percent higher than those of their Vietnamese counterparts. That is partly due to rocketing minimum wages, which are set by local government... As a result, the average minimum wage as a share of the average wage grew from 60 percent in 2008 to around 90 percent in 2018... This discourages hiring, pushing workers into the informal sector, or drives firms to ignore the rules.[87]

Minimum wages aside, labour market regulations may make it more for businesses difficult to fire workers. These kinds of regulations tend to define labour policies in developing countries. The World Bank notes:

> Low- and lower-middle-income economies tend to regulate employment more than do high- and upper-middle-income economies... For example, regulation in the Central African Republic, Madagascar, and Senegal presents significant obstacles for employers hiring new workers or dismissing redundant ones. Among lower-middle-income economies in East Asia and the Pacific, Indonesia is one of the economies with the most rigid employment regulation, particularly on hiring.[88]

These business regulations undeniably contribute to unemployment and depress living standards. A study of 189 countries found a clear relationship between business freedom and poverty. The authors conclude: "We suggest that the conduit for poverty reduction is business creation, both as a source of new jobs and as a manifestation of thriving entrepreneurship."[89] Evidence also shows that onerous labour regulations, designed to protect workers' right and 'help the poor', can end up having a completely counterproductive impact by harming those it precisely intends to help: one study analysed Indian states which had imposed ostensibly 'pro-worker' regulations on manufacturing firms. It was found that these states experienced weaker employment, investment, and productivity growth more urban poverty than the states with less regulation. The study concludes that any attempts to reduce inequalities between workers and business owners, however well-intentioned they may be, may just "end up hurting the poor."[90] Meanwhile, since Indian independence, Bangladesh's labour market has been significantly less regulated than India's – to the country's huge advantage. Between 2010 and 2018 alone, the percentage of the workforce living below the poverty declined from 73.5 percent to 10.4 percent! Much of this is attributable to the growth of the garment sector, which constitutes 53 percent of the country's GDP.[91] Many scholars have argued that this growth took place thanks to Bangladesh's comparatively favourable business environment, namely through a less regulated labour code. The Brookings Institute notes,

> Bangladesh offered a better environment [than India] for manufacturing firms to achieve economies of scale and create a large number of jobs. And though Bangladesh still needs much stronger regulation to protect workers from occupational hazards, the absence of a law that explicitly curtails labor-market flexibility has been a boon for job creation and manufacturing success.[92]

The Need for Freedom

Job creation is an effective medicine for poverty and inequality. A 2006 World Bank study found evidence that growth in labour-intensive sectors is a key driver of poverty alleviation in many countries. Specifically, agriculture, manufacturing, and construction were found to have the greatest anti-poverty effects.[90] Labour market rigidity has certainly been an obstacle to the growth of these sectors in some places. For example, a minimum wage hike in Chile reduced productivity growth in the manufacturing sector.[93] It is clear that for many countries, freeing up labour markets is a highly plausible way to improve living standards. The IMF concluded that substantial labour market deregulation in South Africa could raise incomes by as much as 60 percent and reduce income inequality in the long run, specifying that less advantaged groups, such as the youth, would benefit the most.[94]

CHAPTER 6

Economic Liberalism in Practise

I've argued that economic liberalism, the system of open free trade, strong property rights, and favourable regulatory and tax frameworks, is needed to provide the economic growth which can lift millions out of poverty. We've seen a wealth of longitudinal studies on this topic, most of which confirm that economic freedom yields positive impacts on economic growth. In this chapter, real-world examples of where economic growth has accelerated after governments have pursued liberalisation policies, will be explored

Africa: After decades of stagnation due to the AIDS crisis, in the mid-1990s, economic growth began to accelerate in Africa. This brought concomitant reductions in poverty, illiteracy, and infant mortality.[1]

Economists have devoted much thought to explaining this. The McKinsey Global Institute (MGI) authored a paper in 2010, in which they attributed this to

> [I]mproved political and macroeconomic stability and microeconomic reforms. To start, several African countries halted their deadly hostilities, creating the political stability necessary to foster economic growth. Next, Africa's economies grew healthier as governments lowered inflation, trimmed their foreign debt, and shrunk their budget

deficits. Finally, African governments increasingly adopted policies to energize markets. They privatized state-owned enterprises, reduced trade barriers, cut corporate taxes, and strengthened regulatory and legal systems. Although many governments still have a long way to go, these important first steps enabled a private business sector to emerge.

MGI tested this hypothesis by comparing growth rates in African nations which had made substantial policy changes with those which had not. These countries were split into the broad categories of 'reformers' and 'non-reformers'. The accelerations in GDP growth during the period 2000–2008 over 1990–2000 were observed in both categories. Both enjoyed accelerations, but the reformers enjoyed considerably more: 3.2 percentage points, over the 1.1 percentage points of the non-reformers.[2]

Botswana: Botswana became an independent nation in 1966. In the decades after, it posted some of the highest rates of economic growth in the world. The country had had a laissez-faire upbringing and a strong commitment to private property rights. One study argued that Botswana's strong protection of private property rights exist for basically two reasons. Firstly, its 'precolonial institutions' constrained the power of political elites to expropriate private property. Secondly, the British Empire did little to affect these institutions during the colonial era.[3] Shortly after independence, the country was found to possess rich diamond reserves. Usually, governments would nationalise these resources for the sake of wealth redistribution– but not Botswana. The country's government allowed the main mining company, De Beers, to keep the vast majority of the profits, and later on, liberalised the company's market even further, in exchange for shares in the company and minor influence over the members of the corporate board.[4] On top of that, Botswana privatised its cattle industry. Botswana is one of the economically freest countries on the continent and performs well on ease of doing business by African standards.[5]

Few dispute that Botswana is an African success story. With essentially non-existent infrastructure after independence, the country yet experienced rapid rates of economic growth: from 1965 to 2005, growth averaged at 9 percent per annum.[6] From 1981 to 2019, the share of the population living below $1.90 a day fell from 52 percent to 13 percent.[7]

Rwanda: once a Belgian colony, Rwanda became an independent nation in 1962. There are two major ethnic groups in Rwanda which are relevant here: the Hutus and the Tutsis. There has historically been great tension between them: in the year of independence, armed groups initiated several unsuccessful on the country from Uganda and Burundi. The Hutu-led government retaliated against Tutsi citizens, resulting in the deaths of 12,000 people, and between 40 percent and 70 percent of the Tutsi population fleeing the country. An effort was made in 1964 to remove Tutsis from all positions of political influence – but still many dominated the civil service and education system. In 1973, a coup driven largely by unemployed and disenfranchised Hutus brought the defence minister to the presidency. An economic crisis in the 1980s was worsened by a crash in the world coffee market. The government forced farmers to devalue prices, which predominantly affected Hutus, who occupy the coffee industry. This exacerbated ethnic tensions even further. These growing tensions eventually culminated in a civil war in 1994, in which an estimated 800,000 Tutsis were killed.[8] That same year, incomes halved.[9] The country had been devastated and seemed unlikely to recover economically or socially.

But since 1994, Rwanda has made economic reforms which have put it back on the road to recovery. From 1993 to 2002, the average tariff rate fell from 38.69 percent to 24.21 percent[10]; and during the 1990s, the country's economic freedom index rating rose by two points and is currently the easiest country in Africa to do business.[11] In 1996, the government initiated a large-scale privatisation program and a decade later, 70 of the country's 104 public companies had been sold off. In 2005, TerraCom, the country's main telecommunications company, was privatised: hundreds of miles of fibre optic broadband were laid, and connection prices fell to just a tenth of their 2003 level. In the words of a paper by the OECD,

> The privatisation exercise has increased government revenue and freed up resources. More important, the private sector firms have made huge investments of capital and technical know-how which benefit Rwandans.[12]

Rwanda's long-term economic recovery from the 1994 crisis has been simply astounding. The economy typically grows by up to 9 percent in a single year and poverty continues to plummet, driven by rising farm wages.[13] Once an 'administered' economy, Rwanda has moved heavily towards being a private market system.[14]

Uganda: Uganda obtained independence in October 1962. Immediately, however, political stability collapsed. The prime minister, Milton Obote, introduced a new constitution which drastically increased the power of the executive branch. In 1971, Obote's regime was toppled by military general Idi Amin; once in power, Amin instituted a racist, terrorising regime, expelling most of Uganda's Asian population. Furthermore, he persecuted many ethnic tribes within the country – during his seven years in power, it is reported that up to 500,000 Ugandans were murdered or tortured by his regime. The beginning of the end of Amin's regime was spelt out when he invaded the neighbouring Tanzania in 1978. Along with Obote's private army, Tanzanian troops fought back and reached the capital in April 1979. Obote returned to power in 1980, reimposing himself with violent means. With the civil and economic chaos this caused, he was driven out of power again by general Tito Okello in 1985.[15] This instability wrecked the Ugandan economy. Inflation was sky-high, the private sector was dead, and tax revenues had plummeted. The new government initially proposed a state-centred approach to rebuilding the economy. However, in the end they went down the path of economic liberalisation: foreign exchange markets were liberalised, 75 state-run companies were privatised and in 1987 a major free trade agreement was signed. From 1990 to 2000, Uganda's economic freedom rating more than *doubled*.[16] For 20 years thereafter, growth averaged at 7 percent per year and in 2016 21.4 percent of the population lived below the poverty line, down from 56.4 percent in 1992.[17]

Since Africa is the world's poorest continent, these examples ought to be of particular interest. African countries which still lack the basics of a liberal economy have failed to exhibit impressive rates of growth. The Democratic Republic of the Congo is the most resource-rich country on the continent, even more so than Botswana: its mineral wealth should've turned it into an African success story by now. But this is far from the case. Being one of the least free countries in the entire world, lacking property rights and rule of law, the country has been impoverished by decades of war and corruption.[18]

Now, let's move onto Asia. Asia perhaps contains the most notable neoliberal success stories, the majority of which came into fruition after the Second World War – Hong Kong, Singapore, Japan, Taiwan, and South Korea. However, the three examples we will explore here are more modern: China, India, and Vietnam.

China: from 1949 to 1979, communists ruled China under Marxist revolutionary Mao Zedong. The horrors the Communist Party was responsible for cannot be understated. From 1959 to 1961, 30 million Chinese died in a famine resulting from the Great Leap forward programs. The government had aimed to get the country to rapidly industrialise and multiply crop yields, especially in rural areas. But the abolition of private farming and the forced collectivisation which ensued had the complete opposite effects. Rural life was further inhibited by

The Need for Freedom

the government's anti-rightist campaign and social pressure groups which forced people into political assimilation (those who owned private property were labelled rightists and persecuted).[19]

Mao's rule ended with his death in 1976 and was soon succeeded by Deng Xiaoping. What happened in China afterwards owes itself to Xiaogang, a small village in Anhui Province. As the ownership of private property was not allowed, agriculture operated as rural units – but after the famine had taken place, along with the continuing destitution of most of the population, the farmers of this village made the brave decision to break the law and try something different. In this commune, each family would take ownership of their own property, giving some of what they grew to the government, as was required, but keeping the rest and selling it on a free-market, in total secrecy, of course. The risk was enormous. If any of the farmers were caught by the authorities, they had all agreed that the others would look after their children until the age of 18. Thankfully, this initiative was implemented and for the time being operated unbeknownst to the communist authorities. And it was a radical success. In one-year, agricultural yield increased six-fold and per capita income rose 18-fold.[20] Xiaogang's local economic boom was attracting attention from villages across China. Before long, the central authorities in Beijing had found out what was going on. Had Mao still been in power, these farmers would have unquestionably been prosecuted and brutalised. However, Deng Xiaoping was interested in reforming China, and took inspiration from the Xiaogang model. Nationwide, agriculture was privatised, and alongside that the implementation of a market economy began. Employment in the private sector skyrocketed while employment by the state began to decline precipitously; between 1980 and 2003, China's rating on the economic freedom index rose by 50 percent; from 2006 to 2020, China's ranking on the Ease of Doing Business Index rose from 106th to 31st place; in 2019, China's average unweighted tariff was

2.53 percent, down from 32.17 percent in 1992.[21] The impacts of these reforms have been utterly astounding. Immediately after liberalisation began, growth posted at incredible rates, up to 10 percent each year. Since 1980, incomes have risen almost six-fold while 750 million people have been lifted from extreme poverty.[22]

There is an argument which needs to be addressed, that the miraculous economic growth and poverty alleviation China has experienced cannot be attributed to market liberalisation, but to a dominant state sector which has remained, in the form of high public spending and income redistribution. The data do not support this argument. Firstly, public and social spending is weak in China. With tax take only 22.1 percent of GDP (far below most developed economies and in line with most other poor Asian and Pacific countries), less than 10 percent of GDP is spent on social welfare programs.[23] Meanwhile, it is true that government consumption relative to the whole economy has risen since 1980, during a period of astoundingly high growth. But it also rose steadily in the time before that when growth was much lower. For example, between 1967 and 1984, consumption relative to GDP rose by 4 percentage points. But since 1984, it has risen by barely 2 percentage points.[24] The OECD even remarks of public spending in China:

> a relatively low portion of outlays are made on basic human welfare and development needs, such as education, health, science, and social security. Furthermore, the share of total spending going to education, health, and science has fallen over the last decade. In relation to GDP, public spending on education and health is well below that of nearly all OECD as well as most comparable developing countries, while private spending in these areas is among the highest in the world.[25]

The most dominant forms of government transfers in China are the dibao – agricultural subsidies along with social assistance.

Most dibao recipients have incomes above the poverty line anyway, while most of those in poverty don't receive any social assistance at all![26]

Therefore, government spending does not serve a strong redistributionist function anyway. There is an easy way to prove this further. The Luxembourg Income Study is a thinktank which compiles data on incomes, poverty, and income inequality in many countries. If social spending has a large impact on poverty in a country, we'd expect to see a big disparity between the *pre-tax* poverty rate and the *post-tax* poverty rate. The pre-tax poverty rate computes incomes without any public income transfers factored in, whereas the post-tax poverty rate does add them in. China's 'market income poverty rate' – their pre-tax poverty rate – is 35.5 percent. Their 'disposable income poverty rate' – the post-tax rate – is 26.9 percent. This might sound like a large disparity but is significantly lower than the average of the 49 countries examined (15.4 points).[27] The claim that China's success in alleviating poverty stems from welfare programs and government spending is entirely unfounded.

There is also the argument that deliberate, government-enforced currency devaluations have strongly supported economic growth in China. This is far from clear. While currency devaluations have made Chinese exports cheaper, they have harmed companies who've taken on debt denominated in US dollars. It has also increased the cost of oil to Chinese companies, as it is priced in dollars. This explains the findings of one study which, using data from 1977 to 2006, finds that currency devaluations have had mostly contractionary impacts on the Chinese economy.[28]

It is also true that there has been significant investment into infrastructure in China. Has this had substantial impacts on economic growth? In the words of a 2016 study,

> China is held up as a model to emulate. Politicians in rich democracies display awe and envy of the scale of infrastructure Chinese leaders are able to build. Based on

the largest dataset of its kind, this paper punctures the twin myths that (i) infrastructure creates economic value, and that (ii) China has a distinct advantage in its delivery. Far from being an engine of economic growth, the typical infrastructure investment fails to deliver a positive risk-adjusted return. Moreover, China's track record in delivering infrastructure is no better than that of rich democracies.

The study argues that overinvestment in infrastructure in fact poses long-term economic threats to the Chinese economy. Unproductive projects create a short-term economic boom, but when the expectations of those projects fail to materialise, they become a net economic negative. When projects are financed by government debt, "monetary expansion, instability in financial markets, and economic fragility" result.[29]

In a 2006 article, economist Yasheng Huang argued that China's infrastructural boom only *resulted* from accelerations in economic growth. Large investments only began after growth rates increased:

> In the 1980s, China had poor infrastructure but turned in a superb economic performance. China built its infrastructure after – rather than before – many years of economic growth and accumulation of financial resources. The "China miracle" happened not because it had glittering skyscrapers and modern highways but because bold economic liberalisation and institutional reforms – especially agricultural reforms in the early 1980s – created competition and nurtured private entrepreneurship.[30]

The levels of debt induced by public spending in China have been found to exert a considerably negative impact on economic development. For example, one study found that Chinese cities with more public debt tend to receive less private investment, showing that public spending can 'crowd out' private spending, as will be elaborated upon in a later chapter.[31]

Overall, the view that China's economic growth is state-driven is unsubstantiated. Nicholas Lardy is one of the world's leading experts on the Chinese economy and argues that private sector activity has been by far the most important driver of economic growth in China and calls on the country's government to continue to deregulate and increase competition in the state-dominated sectors of the economy.[32]

It was noted in Chapter 5 that China has made noticeable moves in establishing Special Economic Zones, regions which enjoy more market-oriented economic policies than others. The empirical literature strongly suggests that these Zones have exhibited stronger economic performance than more state-centred regions within China. According to one study, the existence of these Zones has made significant contributions to national economic growth and the introduction of new technologies in the country.[33] Another study found that these Zones tend to attract significantly more investment than their less market-oriented counterparts, and cause workers' real wages to increase; and municipalities with more of these Zones experience these effects to a greater degree than those with fewer.[34]

India: India became independent from British rule in 1947, and from there on was effectively a socialist nation. The economy was dominated by a plethora of state-owned industries, banking was heavily overregulated, and the top marginal tax rate was 97.75 percent, alongside a 3.5 percent wealth tax and a maximum 65 percent corporate tax rate.[35] The collapse of the Soviet Union in 1991 brought down with it the political legitimacy of socialism; reforms to the Indian economy which had been taking place during the 80s picked up speed. The Indian Congress convened, and a series of pro-market policies were enacted: privatisation, banking deregulation, and commercial liberalisation were on the agenda for once: the corporate tax rate came down to 50 percent, financial assets were excluded from the wealth tax and the top marginal tax rate was cut to 40 percent.[36] In the decade after 1990, India's economic freedom rating rose by 1.23 points. From 2015 to 2019, under Prime Minister Narendra Modi, India's GIEO rating rose by six full points, driven largely by business deregulation, FDI liberalisation, and attempts to trim down the size of the country's enormous and inefficient bureaucracy.[37]

These liberalisation reforms have been hugely successful. With a four-fold increase in incomes since 1990, the share of the population living in absolute poverty declined from 45 percent to 20 percent.[38] Furthermore, there has been great improvement in living conditions among India's lowest castes, the Dalits being an example. TV ownership has gone from zero to 45 percent, cell ownership from zero to 36 percent, and the proportion of children eating yesterday's leftovers from 95.9 percent to 16.2 percent.[39] There's no evidence, meanwhile, that this growth phase is only short-term, as it has been sustained well into the 2010s. In 2019, the Indian middle class had 107 million members, three times the size it had been eight years previously.[40]

It is true that India's poverty rate was already declining before the reforms were enacted. However, since the economy has been liberalised, the rate of poverty decline has accelerated considerably, by as much as four-fold since 1991.[41] There is strong evidence that India's growth miracle has been largely driven by liberalisation. A study by Nirupam Bajpai and Jeffrey Sachs found that the subnational states of India which had gone further in implementing reforms had seen higher growth rates, greater FDI inflows, and more impressive improvements in health and educational indicators than states which had lagged in reforms or made them to a lesser extent.[42] Furthermore, some studies have found that in states with less labour market regulation, industries have grown more, providing more jobs and economic opportunity.[43]

Some academics have questioned the effectiveness of certain aspects of liberalisation. A study by economist Petia Topalova found that districts in India which were more exposed to freer trade and international competition saw slower declines in poverty than those which were less exposed. In their own paper, three economists rebutted Topalova's study, pointing out its methodological inadequacies. These flaws had included not controlling for non-tariff barriers on imports, geographical factors, using district-level poverty data instead of state-level data, using inadequate poverty measures, and not giving the dataset enough timespan. Their own analysis, which corrected for all these analytical flaws, came to completely different results from Topalova's original study: states more exposed to foreign competition had in fact experienced *larger* reductions in poverty than those which were less exposed. Additionally, the study found, the benefits of trade liberalisation were more pronounced in states with freer and less regulated labour markets.[44]

The initial delay to these reforms taking place meant that millions suffered. The Cato Institute found that had they been made earlier, an extra 14.5 million children would have survived infancy, 261 million people would have become literate, and 109 million would have risen above the poverty line.[45]

As with China, it might be tempting to attribute India's rise to prosperity to a continued degree of central planning and government investment. This is untrue in many ways.

Firstly, India's still-burdensome regulatory apparatus has undeniably inhibited growth and poverty alleviation. Recall the study mentioned in Chapter 2, which found that restrictions on child labour had in fact caused child labour to become *more* of a problem; recall the study referred to in the previous chapter, which found that labour market rigidity significantly raises employment costs for businesses. Consider also that rampant corruption continues to distort judicial and economic activity.[46]

Secondly, there has been little in the way of income redistribution in India. Just 2 percent of GDP is spent on social welfare programs, even less than in China. And between 1990 and 2020, even factoring in the spending surge which took place during the Covid-19 crisis, there was virtually no increase in government spending relative to GDP, unlike an enormous increase with had taken place in the 20 years preceding 1990, a time of low-growth and economic misery.[47]

The private sector in many places serves as a noticeable substitute for the Indian public sector. A third of students between grades one and twelve attend private schools and in 2018, total consumer spending on education was 350 percent higher than what it was in 2000. For example, Sushil Dhankar runs a low-cost private school in South Delhi, which has 2000 students from four to eighteen (more on this later).[48]

On top of that, the Luxembourg Income Study shows that welfare spending has relatively little impact on poverty in India anyway. India's pre-tax poverty rate is 31 percent, and their post-tax rate is 26.6 percent (data from 2011).[49]

Vietnam: on April 30th, 1975, the final American soldier evacuated Vietnam. It had been a long, brutal war. An estimated 3.3 million Vietnamese had died during the conflict, and whole forests had been obliterated by agent orange, the notorious chemical used by the American military. The two opposing parts of Vietnam, the north and the south, were unified into one communist state. Throughout the late 70s, capitalists were persecuted, government programs forcibly removed people from overcrowded cities, and farming was collectivised. Peasants in the formerly capitalist south often resisted these measures, while the northerners were used to them by now. Thousands fled the country on small, rickety boats, aiming to arrive at the shores of other Southeast Asian nations. One in ten of the 'boat people', as they were known, died out at sea for all sorts of reasons. It took the government a while to realise that the socialist experiment had failed. In the 1980s, alongside China, they began to implement a variety of market-oriented reforms. Collectivisation, for example, was abandoned, and farmers were allowed to operate in a free market. Agricultural production grew significantly, and Vietnam soon became one of the largest producers of rice globally.[50] Growth rates climbed to 8 percent per year, and in 2017, per capita income was ten times what it had been in 1985. Between 2010 and 2016 alone, the number of poor people halved; according to a World Bank report, wage growth has far and away been the biggest driver of poverty reduction in Vietnam, with income transfers accounting for just around 5 percent of the decline. The report notes that wages have risen the fastest in the private sector, driven by very high labour demand, and workers moving out of agricultural jobs.[51] Vietnam is known for its openness to multinational business. The WEF notes:

> [A]rmed with the necessary infrastructure and with market-friendly policies in place, Viet Nam became a hub for foreign investment and manufacturing in Southeast Asia. Japanese and Korean electronics companies like Samsung, LG, Olympus and Pioneer and countless European and American apparel makers set up shop in the country. By 2017, the Financial Times reported, Viet Nam was the largest exporter of clothing in the region and the seconder largest exporter of electronics (after Singapore).[52]

Trade liberalisation has been a strong policy focus as well. Vietnam acceded to the Association of Southeast Asian Nations (ASEAN) in 1995, signed a major trade agreement with the US 5 years later and then joined the WTO in 2007. From 2001 to 2017, tariffs on imports were reduced eight-fold.[53] This has been accompanied by considerable liberalisation of foreign direct investment (FDI) rules. According to the OECD's special measurements, between 1997 and 2020 Vietnam's FDI Regulatory Restrictiveness Index rating fell by 81 percent.[54] It has been found that the provinces in Vietnam which were the most exposed to US tariff cuts under the free trade agreement which was signed experienced faster reductions in poverty and low-skilled workers enjoyed stronger wage growth.[55] Research has also concluded that Vietnam's trade with China has reduced income inequality, as the incomes of the poor have risen the most as a result.[56]

South and Latin America: Free markets were installed in Latin America at the barrels of guns, effectively. The United States backed militias and insurgences which replaced socialist governments with anti-communist dictatorships. Under their watch, a list of ten proposals aimed at liberalising the economies of the region – known as the Washington Consensus – would be implemented. They were intended to ignite long-run economic growth in Latin America. However, to the disappointment of many, they seem to have failed to achieve that. Growth rates remained below their pre-1970s trends for decades after the reforms were put in place, incomes stagnated, and poverty refused to decline. In 2010, researchers at the World Bank tried to counter the general pessimism about the reforms and offered explanations about why growth was so slow after they were enacted. Firstly, they were enacted during a global economic slowdown where, in Latin America especially, inflation was exceptionally high. Growth didn't exactly slow down after the reforms came into place – rather, it remained slow. The Bank's researchers mention a handful of studies finding that in fact Latin America did exceptionally well to return to its pre-1970s growth rates; the reformist governments did brilliant jobs at lowering inflation rates. Secondly, the reforms were not taken to their fullest possible extent. While financial markets were massively deregulated, industries were privatised, and taxes and spending were cut, there were virtually no changes to labour laws, and improving the security of property rights – the backbone of a market economy – was ignored. In fact, the countries which went the furthest with the reforms experienced the best economic outcomes – Chile is an example about to be explored. Thirdly, the researchers argue that financial systems were deregulated too much, making them vulnerable to financial crises which would offset any gains liberalisation elsewhere brought. Finally, it is arguable that Latin America has failed to provide the public commodities which accompany economic growth in a market economy – such as education, infrastructure, and R&D spending (though, some governments are now looking to the private sector to help provide them).[57] As mentioned just now, a few Latin American nations responded incredibly well to economic reforms, partly because they were taken to their fullest extent – Chile being one.

Chile: in 1973, General Augusto Pinochet was installed as military dictator of Chile. I am not writing here to praise him – he was a brutal leader who tortured and murdered his political opponents. However, the long-term economic impacts of the reforms made during his administration cannot be neglected. Chile is by far the freest economy in Latin America and competes in global rankings. From 1975 to 1995, Chile's rating on the index of economic freedom rose by an astounding 3.65 points![58] It is true that Chile endured economic bumps during the liberalisation period, such as a major crisis in 1983 – but this was mostly driven by external shocks, and further liberalisation enabled the economy to recover from this speedily.[59]

Since 1987, Chile's poverty rate has been reduced by 81 percent, and since 1973, per capita income has doubled.[60] Many argue that liberalisation has brought rising income inequality, but the statistics do not support this. From 2013 to 2017, for example, the incomes of the bottom 40 percent of the population grew at 4.9 percent annually.[61]

Other programs which were implemented during the reform the period have also been seen as successful. In 1981, Chile's pensions system was privatised – or, at least, a private-based alternative was created, where workers had the ability to choose between competing private investment managers. Within a year of this occurring, 70 percent of workers had chosen to transition to the private sector options. Within a few years, Chile was running a budgetary surplus and was able to eliminate payroll tax.[62] Other countries, suffering from rising deficits thanks to ever-voracious public pensions programs, could learn from Chile.

Eastern, Southern, and Central Europe: Today, Eastern and Southern Europe is a relatively economically developed region

– but not so long ago, this was not the case. In 1995, the incomes of Estonia, Romania, Georgia, and Lithuania averaged at $4918, the level of many of the least developed countries today.[63] But now, most of them are middle income, if not, high-income countries.

The pain much of the region endured after the collapse of communism cannot be overstated. Estonia, for example, suffered from 30 percent unemployment and a 1000 percent inflation rate. Many therefore argue that Eastern Europe's post-communist depression is evidence that economic liberalisation contains unnecessary reforms. However, this is akin to saying that because drug addicts suffer greatly as they reduce their dependency on drugs, that such transitions were unnecessary. Transition effects may be bad, but that doesn't mean their ultimate outcomes aren't desirable.

There were specific reasons why these collapses occurred. As state-run industries are typically overstaffed, privatisation led to layoffs. Since the public sector constituted such a large portion of the workforce, this caused huge increases in joblessness. Most of communist Europe was dependent on Russia for trade. Understandably, economic turmoil in Russia sent shockwaves throughout the region. And the removal of price controls exposed severe deficiencies in supply, which markets couldn't previously respond to with higher prices. Now that they were, painful readjustments had to occur. Inflation was further augmented by governments being forced to print money in response to significantly reduced revenue intake.[64]

After an awful decade, however, things began to finally turn around for many Eastern and Southern European countries in the 2000s. Inflation subsided, growth took off, and the benefits of liberalisation started to materialise. In Chapter 5, it was established that the effects of privatisations in Eastern Europe are negatively misrepresented. Beliefs about wage cuts and layoffs are mostly unfounded. Here, let's review how some of Eastern Europe has fared.

Estonia: as mentioned, inflation and unemployment peaked at exorbitantly high levels during Estonia's depression. In 1993, Mart Laar was installed as prime minister. Despite presiding over a financial mess, he had only read one book on economics, Milton Friedman's *Free to Choose*. In it, Friedman proposed a flat tax – a single, uniform tax rate for all income levels. Since it had never been implemented before in Europe, Laar decided to give it a go in Estonia. Tax rates were lowered to 26 percent across the board in 1994.[65] Very soon, hearing about the Estonian economic miracle became commonplace: from 1995 to 2005, per capita income grew 2.6-fold, unemployment declined to 8 percent and inflation dropped to no more than 4 percent.[66] Once a communist state, Estonia is now in the top quartile of the economic freedom rankings and wins first place on the International Tax Competitiveness Index, a measure of tax favourability to businesses.[67]

Romania: Romania did not suffer as much as Estonia in the 1990s, but nevertheless endured noticeable economic problems. The unemployment rate peaked at 8.26 percent in 1992 and inflation reached 300 percent in 1995. The proportion of the population living below $5.50 a day also rose nearly seven-fold from 1992 to 1994. The rest of the 1990s and the 2000s brought better years for the country, however: from 1995 to 2005, incomes grew 2.13-fold and extreme poverty returned roughly to its pre-depression levels.[68] Romania is known for its highly favourable tax system to businesses and overall ranking relatively well on the economic freedom index.[69]

Lithuania: in the early 90s, inflation was particularly high Lithuania, peaking at over 1000 percent. But having subsided considerably by 1995, income growth took off, rising 2.45-fold over the next decade.[70] Lithuania ranks 6th on the Tax Competitiveness Index and 11th on the Ease of Doing Business Index.[71]

Georgia: the birthplace of Stalin, Georgia's economy collapsed after the dissolution of the Soviet Union, and on top of that went through a civil war. However, true economic reforms began through the Rose Revolution in 2003 and a series of pro-market policies were enacted. Now, Georgia is one of the freest economies in the entire world and ranks in the top ten in Ease of Doing Business.[72] From 2010 to 2016, poverty was reduced from 35 percent to 10 percent, the size of the middle class tripled and from 2010 to 2015, the incomes of the poorest 40 percent of the population grew at an annual rate of 8 percent.[73]

For those who doubt that GDP per capita is a good metric for living standards, consider another, median disposable income (MDI). This creates an even more positive view of how post-communist Eastern and Southern Europe has fared. For example, between 2011 and 2019 alone, MDI rose by 104 percent in Estonia, 97 percent in Lithuania and 84 percent in Romania (data on Georgia is not available), far above the EU average of 19 percent.[74]

Hourly wage growth has been especially strong in recent years, probably thanks to the region's pro-business environment. Discounting 2020, the year of the Covid-19 pandemic where many countries experienced artificially high wage inflation due to limited workforces, from 2015 to 2019, wages in Lithuania rose by a total of 78 percent, while the EU managed to squeeze out an average of a mere 10 percent. Much of this has been driven by immensely high productivity growth (which tends to dwarf that in other OECD countries).[75]

This certainly does not mean all cases of economic liberalisation have been successful in the long run. In New Zealand, for example, the benefits of liberalisation in the 1980s never really materialised, and employment and growth remained low. However, for decades interest rates were incredibly high in New Zealand, which inhibited economic growth.[76] Another famous example is Russia. After the collapse of the Soviet Union, national assets were sold off en masse under Boris Yeltsin. Most of the buyers were Russian businessowners and foreign bidders were prohibited from competing. As a result of these privatisations, giant monopolies were created. The Soviet Union transitioned from statist communism to a highly and deliberately oligopolistic form of capitalism. Understandably, the benefits of competition never came into fruition. Had Russia allowed more foreign bidders in the privatisation process, perhaps today their economy would be in a better situation.

This chapter has demonstrated that economic liberalisation has consistently acted as a powerful economic stimulus across the world, bringing nations from poverty to prosperity, and transforming the lives of millions of people.

CHAPTER 7

Foreign Aid

Economic freedom is the strongest driver of economic growth. The following chapters will assess whether substantial liberalisation can do the job better than government investment into social welfare, both from domestic and foreign sources. Paternalistic Western philanthropists see large foreign aid programs as the best solutions to poverty and underdevelopment. A handful of economists strongly contest this. In 2014, William Easterly published *The White Man's Burden*, in which he offered refutations of major studies showing a pro-growth effect of international aid. In truth, Easterly's analysis was incredibly superficial. Many studies with similar results have either been published since his book was written or were simply ignored in his writing.

The literature is highly mixed on the growth effects of international aid programs; you could say that there is a 'spectrum' of views these effects, ranging from very positive to negative (including a central 'neutral' position). The table below provides a simplistic outline of each view on the spectrum.

Very Positive:	Aid significantly promotes economic growth regardless of countries' prior economic policies or macroeconomic conditions. The Marshall Plan proves it!
Positive:	Aid promotes growth on the condition that recipients are adopting reasonable economic policies to begin with.
Neutral:	Aid has neither a positive nor a negative impact on economic growth.

The Need for Freedom

| **Negative:** | Aid reduces growth through sustaining corruption and bureaucratic incompetence. |

Very positive: a 2009 study by the IMF observed a 'significant, large and robust' impact of international aid programs on economic growth.[1] A study from the same year published in the *Journal of Economic Development* distinguished the microeconomic and macroeconomic impacts of aid on growth. It first declared that that results of microeconomics are 'clear and encouraging'. But the macroeconomic results were 'inconclusive'.[2] But after analysing a large dataset, the author of the study found that foreign aid still exerts a positive impact on growth. A 2020 study by Elizabeth Adusei examined the impact of foreign on Sub-Saharan Africa's growth rates. It concludes that aid has had a broadly positive impact.[3]

The empirical validity of these studies should not be questioned. However, to any heavily optimistic proponent of international aid initiatives, two things must asked: firstly, can international aid programs increase growth rates more than liberalisation programs? The answer is 'probably not'; aid is in fact a quite inefficient way to boost economic growth. One especially optimistic study found that a 1 percent increase in aid spending relative to the recipients' GDP is associated with a 0.35 percent increase in growth rates.[4] This is unlike, say, trade liberalisation, which is found to boost growth by up to 1.5 percent. Secondly, it is still on the proponents of aid spending to answer why countries which consume international aid are poor in the first place and have failed to achieve at least modest rates of growth.

Strong proponents of aid initiatives for developing countries today may also typically refer to a notable historical example of successful international aid. After the Second World War, the United States enacted the Marshall Aid plan, sending billions of dollars of reconstructive aid to economically devastated European countries. Some credit Europe's miraculous economic recovery from the war to the aid provided. Why can't richer nations now do the same for developing economies? The issue is that there is much scholarly evidence that the Marshall Plan did *not* contribute a lot to Europe's recovery. It ought to be firstly mentioned that aid funding only ever constituted 2.5 percent of recipients' GNP and accounted for less than a fifth of the capital formation during the period of its implementation.[5] Anyhow, there seemed to be little connection between the amount of aid received by countries and the strength of their economic recoveries. The economist Tyler Cowen wrote in an essay in the 1980s:

> [t]hose countries receiving large amounts of aid per capita, such as Greece and Austria, did not recovery economically until US assistance was winding down. Meanwhile, Germany, France and Italy began their recovery before receiving Marshall Plan funds.

The author notes that instead economic policy was a strong predictor of how well countries recovered. Belgium, for example, had kept price controls to a minimum throughout the war anyway, and Germany was quick to undo the strict market regulations left by the Nazi regime. Both received relatively little aid, but one study showed that Belgium had by far the strongest economic recovery in Western Europe.[6] Meanwhile, Germany's recovery simply drew breath from economists: by the end of 1948, German industrial production had already risen to 80 percent of its 1936 levels.[7] These two nations contrast with one of the biggest recipients of Marshall aid, Great Britain, who had a weak recovery compared to some of their European neighbours, despite having been considerably *less* afflicted by the war than many of them. This is perhaps attributable to the economic agenda of Britain's immediate postwar prime minister, Clement Attlee, who nationalised a fifth of the economy, spent vast amounts of money on establishing a universal healthcare program and kept taxes and regulations high. In fact, Britain did not end rationing until 1954.[8] Some scholars argue that the Marshall Plan was not even intended to support economic growth in Europe but served political purposes. Historian Albrecht Ritschl writes,

> The allocation of aid often seemed to follow political, not economic needs: nearly half the resources never arrived in the disaster areas on the former European battlefields but served to buy political support in England and France, and to fend off communist threats in various countries.

This does not mean that Marshall aid had *no* impact on recoveries; some research has found that it helped stimulate specific economic sectors, which contributed to economic recovery.[9] But it is baseless to claim that overall economic recovery in Europe was strongly motivated by Marshall aid.

Positive: generally, the positive literature on aid argues that initiatives can boost growth, but provides a few caveats: for example, that recipient nations can only benefit from aid spending if they pursue robust macroeconomic policies, or that aid can be beneficial in the long run, but has negative short-term affects, or that the benefits of aid will disappear beyond a certain spending threshold. Let's explore some of these studies:

- The Centre for Economic Development and International Trade (CREDIT) published a study with results which 'strongly support' the view that foreign aid impacts growth positively to an extent. Importantly, however, it warns that this is 'conditional only a stable macroeconomic policy environment'.[10]
- A study of 95 different countries gave a quite diluted opinion of the benefits of aid. It found a 'U-shaped relationship' between aid spending and growth. Initially, aid exerts a negative impact on growth, but after a while, its influence becomes positive. Moreover, the study specifies that foreign direct investment (FDI)

and population are far greater determinants of growth (and there is even some evidence that aid can displace FDI inflows). Meanwhile, the study submits that 'strengthening [the] legal frameworks' would be vastly important for developing countries, while also pointing out that 'overdependency on the influx of Official Development Assistance (ODA) might lead to negative impacts on [the] growth as a whole'.[11]
- A study by the economist David Dollar, who we met in the first chapter, found that aid can exert a positive force on growth *if and only if* recipients are adopting reasonable institutional and macroeconomic policies to begin with.[12]

With much of this research in mind, any reasonable person will ask 'what are the policies which need to accompany aid inflows to boost economic growth?'. The argument of this book is that it is significant economic liberalisation.

Neutral: a large body of academic research finds that international aid initiatives exert neither positive nor negative influences on the recipient countries' economic growth rates:

- In his 2014 book, William Easterly examined a large group of countries over the period 1951 to 2001. He placed them into two categories: those which had received above average levels of aid relative to GDP, and those which had received below average. Easterly found no difference in the growth rates of each category over that period. According to him, this suggests that aid has neither positive nor negative statistically discernible impacts on growth.[13]
- Of course, these data suffer the bias that aid tends to go to poorer countries, or to countries which are experiencing weak growth anyway. According to a 2005 study by the IMF, however, even after correcting for

this bias, aid is not found to exert a positive or negative impact on economic growth.[14]
- A study of 16 West African countries from 1996 to 2017 found that overall aid exerts a neutral influence on economic growth; however, the study also specified that any negative impact that foreign aid could've had been mitigated by institutional variables, such as trade openness. Therefore, to impact growth rates, the study recommended 'building formidable economic, social and political institutions.'[15]
- Another study analysed 97 countries over the period 1974 to 2013. It was found that aid has a 'positive but insignificant' influence upon economic growth. This is probably because while the study found that aid increases consumption and investment, it decreases exports, so there were little net economic gains.[16]

The final study mentioned essentially encapsulates one of the largest reasons why aid initiatives may fail to help recipient countries economically. The truth is, aid can infect recipients with the notorious Dutch Disease: despite higher levels of growth and consumption, aid investments increase exchange rates between poor and rich countries, thereby *reducing exports*. As trade is an important means of growing weaker economies, this negative externality of aid programs can pose a significant challenge to poverty alleviation.

Negative: the view that international aid programs negatively impact economic growth relies on individual case study, admittedly, and not big longitudinal datasets. But the lessons learned from these examples can nevertheless be useful:

- Throughout the 1970s, Tanzania received large aid inflows, yet poverty, low growth and high budget deficits persisted. A study examined the Tanzanian

economy from 1976 to 2014 and concluded that aid had exerted a negative impact on economic growth.[17]
- After becoming independent in 1962, Zaire (now the Democratic Republic of the Congo) received considerable amounts of international aid. It was eventually discovered that the nation's president, Mobutu Sese Seko, was expropriating these funds for his own personal enrichment. Thanks to decades of corruption, and resultant wars, the DRC is one of the poorest countries on the planet.[18]
- EU-provided farm subsidies to Ireland discouraged rural-urban migration. Since labour productivity is so much higher in the cities, these subsidies inhibited economic growth.[19]
- Since aid flows into generally corrupt developing countries, there is evidence that it provides fuel for corrupt and incompetent bureaucracies, which mismanage resources and put burdens on the economy.[20]

Regardless of what view of international aid you subscribe to, none of the literature, even highly positive, would suggest that aid is the best way to stimulate economic growth in developing nations. Recall the most optimistic study by far found that a 1 percent increase in aid spending relative to GDP increases growth rates by 0.35 percent. This is pathetic compared to the results of a World Bank study mentioned earlier, that a 1-point increase in economic freedom can raise growth rates by 1 percentage point annually.

The very positive view of aid is perhaps overly optimistic. It is true that as aid investments flow in, exchange rates are affected, such that exports are depressed. The neutral view of aid appears to the most academically plausible. If not, then it may well be just the positive view. However, in that scenario, the focus ought not be increasing aid spending, but asking what the correct macroeconomic policies for fostering economic growth and absorbing aid spending are in the first place.

CHAPTER 8

The Efficacy of Public Spending (and Labour Unions too!) In Alleviating Poverty

It is widely accepted that government spending is necessary to sustain economic growth. Without basic physical, social, and human infrastructure, economies cannot function, and poverty cannot fall.

This does not mean, however, that government spending will positively impact growth in all circumstances. The effectiveness of spending has been found to be dependent on other economic variables, such as national indebtedness, exchange rate flexibility, and openness to free trade. A major study found that the multiplier impacts of government spending/ consumption (meaning how much additional value it creates in the long run through boosting economic growth) are different on developed and non-developed economies. In developed economies, the multiplier effect is 0.39, meaning for every dollar of government consumption, 39 cents of additional output are created. In non-developed economies, however, the effect is *-0.03*, meaning for every dollar consumed, 3 cents are *lost* in economic output.[1] This may be for various reasons. Some evidence shows, for example, that government spending can reduce output because if it financed by deficits, there is less money available for private sector borrowing, due to higher interest rates. A 2016 report by the US Congressional Budget Office (CBO) explains this in greater detail:

> CBO's central estimate is that for each dollar that the federal deficit increases, domestic private investment falls by 33 cents. That reduction in private investment results in a smaller capital stock, eventually shrinking output. Similarly, a reduction in federal borrowing leaves more money available for private investment, resulting in a larger capital stock and eventually greater output.[2]

Hence, as explored earlier in the case of China, government spending can 'crowd out' private investment, negating any positive economic impacts that government investment might yield. According to one analysis of the literature, by economists Nihal Bayraktar and Blanca Moreno-Dodson, the link between public spending and economic growth is tenuous (unlike for economic freedom and growth). The study specified that where public spending does benefit growth, countries must have stable macroeconomic conditions in the first place.[3] Ironically, as we shall see in the next chapter, excessive spending can induce destabilising macroeconomic environments. It may be logical to conclude that public spending, while necessary and important for development, can only maximise its growth-boosting effects when relatively low in the first place.[4]

Further research has expressed pessimism at the idea that significant public investment is the key to solving underdevelopment. A study by Andrew Warner, who co-authored many research papers with Jeffrey Sachs, of 124 low- and middle-income countries over a 50-year period found that the relationship between spending and growth is weak and inconclusive. Damningly, Warner wrote in his paper, "there is no robust evidence that the investment booms exerted a long-term positive impact on the level of GDP." Warner addresses claims that large-scale public spending programs were responsible growth miracles in cases such as Korea, Japan, and Taiwan – growth in fact had begun to accelerate before major programs were implemented. For other famous cases, like China and Vietnam, Warner argues that agricultural liberalisation was responsible for explosions in growth (and besides, spending programs took up relatively small portions of the economy anyway).[5]

Economists frequently recommend high investment into physical infrastructure – building roads, bridges, and waterways – as a key solution to igniting economic growth and solving global poverty. Developing nations, which tend to have much weaker infrastructural amenities than richer ones, are assumed to benefit massively from investment in infrastructure. The literature, however, is even divided as to whether these investments do stimulate long-run development. One study found that, although investments in physical infrastructure do generally *on average* boost long-run economic growth, there is massive variation in this effect across the world. According to these findings, infrastructure spending can't be used as a particularly *reliable* booster of growth.[6]

Investment in social welfare programs is promised to improve national 'social indicators' – such as life expectancy, infant mortality, literacy, and so forth. One of the most comprehensive pieces of research on the relationship between public spending and social indicators comes from economist Paulo Silva Lopes. In a study for the IMF, he found either weak or absent correlations between social welfare spending as a percentage of GDP in various sub-Saharan African countries and indicators – whether they be life expectancy, infant mortality, literacy, or the availability of teachers in schools and doctors in hospitals. This should strongly cast doubt on the claim that substantial public investment into health, education, and general welfare alone is the best policy to improve national social outcomes.[7]

Public spending programs are sometimes channelled through state-run companies or bureaucracies. Seeing that they tend to be particularly inefficient (especially in developing countries), these programs can conceivably be wasteful and incompetent. For example, there were various public sector efforts in Asia and

Africa to boost agricultural mechanisation through an array of subsidies. These are widely seen as having failed. One review of 38 mechanisation programs in 21 countries found that only two were deemed successful. The reason for the failure of these programs, the study notes, is that "[t]here is a risk that a subsidized program can restrain the machinery supply from the private sector, which makes the program often unsustainable."[8]

The main purpose of this chapter, however, is not just to explore whether public spending enhances economic growth or not and achieves its aims. It is mainly to question the view that increased government spending itself is the best way to improve social services, such as the delivery of infrastructure, healthcare, and education. Clearly, the public sector must play a role in implementing these services. However, they must be made efficient and practical – which bureaucracies are bad at ensuring. It is essential that developing nations focus on how money is spent on these services, not the amount of money which is initially invested.

There is no doubt that social welfare programs are necessary, to an extent, to alleviate poverty. However, as we have seen in previous chapters, poverty has declined in many developing economies, as it did in the West, independently of significant government spending. In Chapter 1, a meta-analysis of 19 empirical studies was mentioned, which showed that public welfare initiatives have played miniscule roles in the immense poverty reductions which have taken place in low- and middle-income countries. Overall, research finds that, far and away, *economic growth is the most powerful tool to alleviate poverty*. Focusing on growth maximisation is a much better way to help the poor than focusing on redistribution.

In fact, in many developing countries, welfare programs have only begun to help the poor after economic growth has done much of the heavy lifting. An analysis of poverty reduction in Kazakhstan over the period 2001–2009 argued that economic growth was the 'main driver' of the reduction in the first half of the decade, but redistribution began to help out in the second half.[9] A study of rural China, which has contributed to much of the world's decline in poverty in the 40 years before the Covid crisis, found that economic growth was the largest driver of poverty alleviation. Anti-poverty social programs, the author notes, have been "effective, but not efficient."[10] Inefficient public spending can induce higher tax rates and/or deficits, both of which reduce economic growth, the main engine of poverty alleviation.

Social Welfare

There have been concerns about the efficiency of how welfare spending reduces poverty. In 2016, Sean Higgins and Nora Lustig studied welfare states in 17 developing countries and concluded that, undoubtedly, they had helped alleviate poverty. However, large segments of the poor population had nevertheless fallen deeper into poverty, because the taxes raised needed to fund these spending programs had meant they were paying more than they were receiving in income support. In fact, in more than half the countries analysed, at least a quarter of the poor population had lost income because of the welfare programs in use.[11]

Welfare spending is practically non-existent in many developing countries, but there a few have implemented noticeably robust programs: Brazil is a classic example. The country's redistribution initiatives, known as the Bolsa Família programs, which have been operational since 2003, have received enormous praise. Despite the praise they receive, however, the literature is mixed on how successful these programs have been successful. As one researcher notes, studies tend to credit them with reducing poverty in Brazil only by between 0.15 and 1.88 percentage points.[12] Moreover, over the period 2000–2014, when the programs were drastically expanded, other South and Latin American countries saw even greater declines, including Peru, Colombia, Bolivia, and Ecuador, where social welfare spending as a percent of GDP was in fact lower.[13] While the literature suggests that redistributionism played an important role in the alleviation of poverty and compression in incomes in the region during the 1990s and 2000s, recall the earlier study by the IMF, mentioned in the first chapter, which demonstrates that the growth of commodity prices in the 2000s was strongly associated with poverty reduction. More worryingly, though, some warn about the long-term fiscal impacts of Bolsa Família: researcher Anthony Hall warns that the program's continuous expansion could induce severe dependency of recipients. More so, he points out that there is evidence that welfare transfers are diverting money away from other social institutions, like investment in sanitation, housing, and education.[14]

Proponents of the efficacy of welfare initiatives tend to cherry-pick case studies. While Brazil's experience with welfare spending has been relatively good, other less successful examples are neglected. Mexico is a little-known case study: in the 1990s, President Enrique Peña Nieto, unveiled Prospera, which has given cash transfers to Mexico's poor since. It is difficult to evaluate whether these programs have worked or not. Since then, Mexico's economy has been through a lot – a severe recession in 1994, another in the early 2000s, the displacement of 4.9 million Mexican farming families thanks to the importation of subsidised US corn, and persistently high inflation. However, arguments for social welfare tend to hold that these programs can raise the poor's incomes even in the face of extreme economic adversity. In Mexico, this has not been the case. According to certain metrics, poverty has only declined since 1996 thanks to the economy's recovery from the prior recession. But nevertheless, there has been little net decline since 1992, when programs were operational. For example, in 1992, 53.1 percent of Mexico's population were "unable to afford food, healthcare, education, clothing, housing and transportation." In 2014, that was 55.1 percent. So, in fact if we use this specific measure, poverty rose slightly! Even if we are generous, and use a later date as a starting point, from when a greater decline took place, the programs' success is still far from vindicated. Other countries in Latin America, where social expenditure is often far lower, experienced sharper reductions in poverty than Mexico, even if different measures of poverty are used. From 1994 to 2014, the percentage of Mexico's population living in extreme poverty fell to 41.2 percent from 45.1 percent. The rest of Latin America, excluding Mexico, experienced a decline five times faster, from 46 percent to 25 percent.[15]

Chile's conditional cash transfer program, Solidario, is fairly well-known. Studies are divided on its success. For example, according to one study, in the short term, Solidario has failed to make significant inroads into poverty. This does not mean that the program could not be more beneficial longer run; but the lack of positive short-run effects should bring into doubt the cost-effectiveness of this particular program.[16]

Outside Latin America, researchers provide examples of the success of welfare initiatives – Tunisia, Tanzania, and Sri Lanka as a few examples.[17] However, they tend to ignore a large exception to their argument, Ghana. Academic analysis has found that Ghana's notably progressive tax structure and redistribution programs do little to impact poverty. In fact, as one study notes, "were it not for the in-kind benefits from health and education spending, the overall effect of government spending and taxation would actually increase poverty in Ghana."[18]

The reasons why welfare spending may fail to alleviate poverty require greater elaboration. Some sociologists have primarily attributed this to a kind of 'displacement effect': in order to qualify to receive publicly provided income transfers, recipients are forced to reduce their private income obtained through job earnings and family membership. This is because of how welfare states are usually designed: when recipients begin to earn private income, their welfare transfers are reduced. As a result, welfare spending has been found to incentivise higher levels of worklessness and single parenthood.

For example, a 1998 study from the United States found that a 50 percent increase in welfare benefits increases the rate of single parenthood by 43 percent[19]; and a $1 increase in benefits reduces private earnings by $0.67.[20] The welfare state in its current form is a truly inefficient way to alleviate poverty – and developing countries must be cautious not to replicate it when they have reached the economic maturity to begin implementing large-scale social welfare programs. Another negative consequence of Western-style welfare states is a reduction in the savings rate, because social services eliminate the need for private wealth accumulation. A study by the European Central Bank found a negative correlation between welfare spending and household net wealth. Although they're credited with reducing *income* inequality, they have the rarely mentioned effect of producing "an increase – rather than a decrease – of observed wealth inequality."[21] The national savings rate can have a noticeable influence on economic growth. Savings can stimulate investment, remittances, production, and employment by making capital more available. A study of Kosovo, using data from 2007 to 2017, found that deposits had had a strongly positive influence on growth.[22] A similar study done on Botswana came to the same conclusion.[23] A 2010 study found that in both developed and developing countries, there is a moderately robust relationship between the national savings rate and the size of GDP.[24] It is a mistake to promote policies which reduce national savings and capital accumulation.

What would be a more efficient welfare system which wouldn't have such negative side effects? To answer this, policymakers in the developing world must seek to maintain the connection between poverty reduction and economic growth as economies reach higher levels of development, which systems in rich nations fail to do because they incentivise worklessness and single parenthood. Evidence suggests that two fundamental factors can broadly convey the benefits of growth to low-income households in developed countries: full-time employment and marital partnership. Only 2 percent of full-time workers in the United States live below the poverty line, and only 4 percent of married couples do. This is opposed to 26 percent for those who worked less than a week in one year and 22 percent for female-headed households, and 12 percent for male-headed ones. In fact, the median household income of married couple families is more than twice that of female-headed ones, and 50 percent higher than that of male-headed ones.[25] The great reductions in poverty before the 1960s occurred in part thanks to high and stable marriage and employment rates, which allowed the benefits of productivity growth, translating into higher wages, to affect a large majority of the population. The rise of single parenthood and the decline in employment rates among poorer families have offset the advantages economic growth has brought to them. In fact, the economist Isabelle Sawhill argues that had the proportion of children living in single parent homes in 1998 been equal to its 1970 level, child poverty would have been 4.4 percentage points lower.[26] Her research at the Brookings Institute showed that increasing marriage rates and full-time employment (as well as raising high school attendance and reducing family size) could reduce the US poverty rate by 72 percent (as opposed to only 8.5 percent, under *the doubling of welfare benefits*).[27] It is probably because of the negative factors which welfare spending induces that the poverty-reducing capacity of welfares spending in the United States was quickly exhausted, as some research has showed.[28]

Developing countries will need to preserve these same vehicles so economic growth can continue to alleviate poverty and raise median incomes in the long-term.

There are different ways to ensure the efficiency of welfare transfers, to limit their possible negative side effects. For example, income transfers could be made conditional in poorer countries – meaning families receive them only for fulfilling certain criteria, such as educating their children or entering the workforce.[29] Similarly, welfare reforms in the United States in 1996, which required poor welfare recipients to work a specified number of hours, drastically reduced poverty and increased the employment rates of poor single mothers.[30] If transfers are unconditional, they could potentially subsidise idleness and delay the alleviation of poverty. Importantly as well, welfare programs should not discriminate on any geographical basis. For example, the poorest of the global poor tend to live in rural areas. It may be tempting for policymakers to support giving additional government transfers to stimulate poverty alleviation and economic development in rural areas. These could come in the form of farm subsidies, for example. However, this could incentive the recipients of those additional transfers to remain in rural areas, thereby discouraging rural-urban migration. Since urban areas are so much more productive than rural ones, this could limit economic growth in the long run. Some research has suggested that Ireland's economic was held back by EU transfers, because heavy farm subsidies gave people incentives to remain in unproductive rural communities. The Irish economy didn't begin to accelerate, and thus reduce poverty, until those subsidies were withdrawn, and liberalisation reforms were implemented.[31]

Across the world, a welfare policy proposal which is gaining in popularity is the Universal Basic Income (UBI). The program involves a unitary, unconditional income transfer to all households below a certain income threshold. Many scholars, such as Charles Murray, recommend this as a replacement with the overly bureaucratic welfare systems of most Western countries. This is in contrast to conditional cash transfers, where recipients receive money conditional on them doing certain things – like sending their children to school or getting jobs. The efficacy of basic incomes in developing nations has been investigated relatively little by scholars. There is a handful of studies available, however, which cast doubt on the poverty-reducing powers of the UBI within the developing world. A study published in 2018, using data from Indonesia and Peru, found that targeted transfers are far better than basic incomes at reducing poverty because poor households receive larger budgetary support.[32] A study from Brazil found that, initially, basic income programs do reduce poverty. However, in the long run they lead to increases in poverty, because recipients send their children to school less, work less, and save less. The study then found that conditional cash transfer systems outperform basic incomes in almost every way: they reduce poverty and inequality far more effectively, as well as increasing overall recipient welfare much more. This is mostly because conditional transfers force recipient households to keep their children in school, therefore significantly benefitting their long-term economic prospects.[33] Clearly, the UBI is an inadequate policy for poverty-alleviation compared to conditional transfers.

There are potential private sector initiatives which can complement state-funded welfare programs. In the 1990s, Muhammed Yunus set up the Grameen Bank: a microcredit scheme, where people who'd be too poor to afford normal bank loans would get principal loans at discounted rates. This put capital within the reach of the poor entrepreneurs. The success of microcredit schemes – or microfinance, as it is sometimes called – in alleviating poverty is heavily contested. Some research has even found that the schemes had had no impact on the incomes of the borrowers whatsoever.[34] But according to Microcredit Summit Finance, from 1990 to 2008, the microcredit scheme pulled 10 million Bangladeshis out of poverty.[35] Considering the tepid and disputed successes of Brazil's, Mexico's, and Chile's welfare programs, this seems vastly impressive. In particularly scathing language, author Mark Skousen writes:

> In less than three decades, Yunus and his Grameen Bank have done more to alleviate extreme poverty than [the] entire $2.3 trillion in wasted foreign aid programs.[36]

Labour Unions

How would increasing levels of worker unionisation affect public welfare in developing countries? Many economists, such as Paul Krugman, attribute the sharp rise in American living standards during and after the Second World War to a militant labour movement which lobbied for higher wages.[37] For various theoretical and historically obvious reasons, this could not have been the case: unions raise wages by limiting the supply of labour, thus inducing unemployment. Unfortunately, this fell disproportionately on racial minorities, and white unions tried their best to forcibly exclude African Americans from the labour market. The same was a problem in apartheid South Africa, where white unions would behave similarly to exclude the Black population from employment.[38]

Empirical studies have attempted to quantify the economic impacts of unionisation. An analysis of 183 European regions over the period 1980 to 2003 confirmed the suspicion that unions reduce employment and total economic growth.[39] South Africa's unemployment rate currently tops 30 percent, and three quarters of young people are unable to find work. Researchers have found that the country's highly rigid labour market, enforced by powerful labour unions, are a strong contributor to the unemployment crisis.[40] To achieve first-world living standards, emerging countries must remain attractive to first-world industries and levels of capital investment. Raising the costs of labour, unions have often removed these incentives. Many attribute the collapse of Detroit City's auto industry to labour unions. Raising labour costs, car prices thus rose – and buyers began to consumer cheaper Japanese cars. Once an economic powerhouse, Detroit is now a deindustrialised city.[41] We saw in a previous chapter that Bangladesh built itself to prosperity with a relatively unregulated labour market free of labour unions which could have reduced the country's attractiveness to foreign investment. This enabled Bangladesh's garment industry to flourish, pulling millions from poverty as a result. India, on the other hand, was ensconced in labour unions as well as significant regulation. This contributed enormously to the country's decades of economic and industrial stagnation.

Naturally, labour unions can massively harm consumer welfare – in fact, from 1935 to 1950 Americans saw coal prices more than double, the coal industry being heavily unionised, while natural gas prices rose by no more than 10 percent, the industry being significantly freer from organised labour.[42] Consumers may be just as poor as the workers fighting for higher pay. If vital commodities are made more expensive as a result of higher labour costs, poverty alleviation could be impeded due to declining real wages. In fact, union bargaining was arguably a strong contributor to the stagflation of the 1970s in richer countries (a period of low growth and high inflation). Whenever prices rose, unions would compel employers to raise wages to keep up with inflation. But higher labour costs would be offset by higher prices – which unions would respond to by lobbying for higher pay, and so forth.[43] In a particularly scathing study, Richard Vedder and Lowell Gallaway wrote that labour union presence had reduced US economic output by the trillions of dollars, such as by hampering employment and virtually bankrupting various industries.[44]

Overall, there has been relatively little research into the economic impacts of labour unions on developing economies. However, one study examined six Latin American countries and found that while they may have a very slight positive impact on productivity (although it is some cases negative), this is not nearly enough to offset the effects of higher union wages. Therefore, the study found that among these countries, unionisation was negatively related to investment in capital and R&D spending, both of which are crucially catalysts for economic development.[45] A study of Brazilian businesses found that unions reduce firm profitability. The relationship between unionisation and firm productivity was found to be more complicated; with initial increases in unionisation from a low-level, there are concomitant increases in productivity.

However, beyond a certain point, productivity begins to decline.[46] A study of the Guatemalan coffee industry found that the presence of unions reduces the productivity of land per worker significantly.[47]

Unions are seen as important means to maintain workers' rights, but as we saw in the second chapter, considerable reductions in child employment, working hours, and even workplace deaths occurred in the relative absence of influential labour unions (as well as significant government regulation). The most effective way to increase workers' living standards is to enable economic and productivity growth, as well as maintaining a relatively competitive labour market. Unions have been demonstrated by various case studies to reduce employment growth, increase consumer prices, damage the competitiveness of industries, and reduce business investment in capital and R&D. This has the risk of reducing the living standards of the rest of the population and placing a considerable barrier to economic growth in developing nations.

Physical Infrastructure

In this chapter, the evidence has already been presented that investment in infrastructure is not necessarily a reliable way to boost growth in developing economies. That is not the point of this part of the chapter, though. It is to investigate how private sector businesses can help develop infrastructural amenities in the developing world, and the various barriers which exist to that.

When many Western nations were still developing, large-scale infrastructure projects were conducted by private businesses. James. J. Hill, for example, famously constructed a railroad from Michigan to Washington state in the absence of any federal subsidy.[48] The history of the telegraph also illustrates this point well. The telegraph was invented in 1836 and the United States Congress would oversee its development.

This was financially disastrous. In 1845, expenditures on the telegraph exceeded revenues by a ratio of six to one. The bureaucrats who administered this project were propped up by taxpayers' subsidy. When they failed, the money they lost was not their own. Reluctantly, Congress privatised the telegraph the following year. After that, it took off. As economic historian Burton Folsom writes:

> Finally, in the hands of entrepreneurs, the telegraph business expanded immediately. Telegraph promoters showed the press how it could instantly report stories occurring hundreds of miles away. Bankers and stock-brokers saw how they could live in Philadelphia and invest daily in New York. Even policemen used the telegraph to catch escaped criminals. As the quality of service improved, telegraph lines were strung all over the settled portions of the country.

In 1847, two major companies were competing for business in the Northwest Territory. One of these businessmen was F. O. J. Smith. With his entrepreneurship in the Northwest having been a tremendous success, in 1866, private investors gave Smith the capital to string wires all across the Atlantic.[49]

The West's earlier infrastructural development was fuelled strongly by private investment – and the same is happening in many emerging economies. MGI's 2010 report notes that Africa's infrastructural amenity which grew the fastest by far from 2000 to 2008 was telecommunications. In fact, access to telecoms rose almost 19-fold over that period. In total, 62 percent of Africa's telecoms investment was private. This is unlike other amenities, which received considerably less private investment as a share of total investment over the same period, and grew much more slowly – namely, power and water utilities.[50] The following case study elucidates this about telecoms very well. In 1998, the 55 million inhabitants of the DRC had only 3000 telephones among them. That year, Mo Ibrahim, a Sudanese-born British entrepreneur, set up Celtel, which had 800 employees at the time. Unlike many of his colleagues, Ibrahim saw great investment opportunities in Africa and in the early 2000s spent significant amounts of capital on building cellular communications networks throughout the continent. There were many challenges – the absence of roads meant that materials had to be transported by helicopter. At first, costs to consumers were incredibly high, at over $3 per minute of phone call. This was in part because African governments are so protective of their borders, so it was very difficult to establish a microwave link between the DRC and its neighbouring Congo. After two whole years of negotiating with both governments, this was finally permitted, and costs fell to just 28 cents per minute. The week that rate was offered for the first time, telephonic communication between the two countries rose seven-fold.[51]

Elsewhere, telephone access has been increased by privatisation. In Brazil, before privatisation, telephones took years to obtain, and only for exorbitant prices. Put simply, they were a luxury of the rich. Within eight years after privatisation, however, prices had shot down and telephone access had risen five-fold.[52]

Burdensome regulations and inefficient bureaucracies reduce the incentives for private investors to invest in African infrastructure. In fact, 85 percent of Africa's utilities hold their prices below the levels required to cover total costs.[53] Deregulation of utilities would provide a huge boost to their development. A dataset of 40 developing countries over a decadal period found that enforcing property rights and reducing bureaucratic obstructiveness significantly incentivise private investment into infrastructure projects.[54]

Good-quality airports and air transportation systems are vital components of infrastructure, and they tend to be deficient in emerging economies.

The literature suggests that privatisation is a good way to improve the quality of airports. A review of 201 airports in 67 different countries found that privatisation significantly improves managerial quality and responsiveness to passenger needs.[55] On top of that, the deregulation of air travel and airline companies has been shown to significantly benefit consumers, both in high-income and low-income countries. Air travel is one of the most regulated industries in the world; as research by the International Transport Forum concluded, the number of competing firms in the market balloons after liberalisation. Inefficient and unpopular airlines go bankrupt and low-cost airlines enjoy amazing growth.[56] Based on data from North America and a few European countries, one study found that airline liberalisation led to a 40 percent reduction in fares while access to flights expanded considerably.[57] Unfortunately, as with many other sectors of the economy, air travel is tightly regulated in developing countries. On the brighter side, some have gone in the direction of liberalisation, with impressive results. Pakistan, for example, modified a 1972 agreement signed with Saudi Arabia, which tried to limit competition between airlines. Afterwards, the number of competitors in the market rose impressively and by 2013, consumers had saved a total of $60 million since 2008. Consumers have had similar experiences in Mexico and Southern Africa, where fares on liberalised air routes declined on average by a fifth.[58] Policymakers should seriously consider widespread air travel deregulation to boost investment into developing economies.

Housing is the most important element of infrastructure. High housing costs are problems which afflict both rich and poor countries. In poorer ones, unaffordable housing results in slum formation, subjecting millions to appalling living conditions. Across the world, zoning regulations have been found to be a particularly strong driver of housing costs. Many studies have focused on the United States, where the extent of regulations vary between states and localities. One study found that a one deviant point increase in land-use regulations increases housing costs by 22 percent.[59] Further literature suggests that zoning deregulation could lower homelessness in the United States significantly.[60] A major study of 211 cities in 27 developing countries found that regulations are a strong driver of costs, because they restrain the supply of housing so that it cannot meet demand. To encourage the private sector to compete more in the rental markets of developing economies, the study recommends the introduction of an array of financial incentives.[61]

Zoning regulations have contributed massively to slum formation. Formal land is so expensive to buy because of regulations, that developers instead construct far cheaper informal housing. A study published in 2019 found that, together, significant zoning deregulation and cuts to property tax could reduce slum formation by 30 percent.[62] The research also noted that slum expansion cannot be attributed to any kind of specific policy – but rather due to migration into the cities from rural areas. Any well-meaning attempts to improve the quality of slums should be approached with caution, the study argues, as they sometimes have unintended impacts. In fact, a study from Brazil found that slum upgrades were often followed by slum expansions, because they became more attractive to rural people who subsequently migrated to them.[63] From my perspective, this isn't necessarily a bad thing, as migration to urban areas brings a huge increase in living standards in emerging economies. But those who are against slums because of their aesthetic displeasure ought to be opposed to regulatory measures to improve the quality of slums.

Rent controls is a popular way to make housing more affordable to the poor. But this is a classic, well-intentioned policy which has completely counterproductive and harmful effects. As the laws of supply and demand dictate, when the price of a commodity is held below its market value, shortages of it result. Mumbai is an excellent example of this happening, a city which has had strict rent control policies since the 1940s, where as a result 95 percent of the housing which has been constructed since has been for ownership, the remaining 5 percent for rentiers.[64] Of course, rent control has negatively impacted the quality of housing as well. In 2010, the World

Bank published a book arguing that because of such, landlords had less of an incentive to invest in maintaining the safety and durability of homes, causing their extreme vulnerability during the monsoon seasons.[65]

Education

Education is more than vital to securing economic growth, by raising national human capital levels and thus increasing worker productivity. The typical assumption is that significant public investment is the best way to improve the quality of schools, and that investment needs to be especially high in developing economies. This is a misconception. Although lower in per pupil terms, Africa's spending on education as a percent of GDP is about equal to the OECD's (besides, education spending takes up a much larger share of African government budgets than in higher income countries). And more importantly, the correlation between education spending and actual academic outcomes in developing nations is much weaker than commonly expected; MGI notes:

> African countries could get more from their current education spending. For example, Morocco spends about the same amount per capita on education as Thailand, yet has much lower student scores. Similarly, Botswana's per capita education spending is comparable to South Korea's (not including private spending), yet the scores of Botswana students lag far behind those of South Korean students. Studies show that simply adding teachers or other resources to schools in developing countries is not always enough to improve student learning.[66]

Improving services doesn't necessarily come through increasing spending on them; in Indonesia, a law mandates the government to spend a fifth of its budget on education. About half of those who complete school are illiterate.[67] Improvements in the quality of services only comes through competition between firms in a market environment. How can this be applied to education? A model which is becoming increasingly popular among economists is the system of 'voucher schools'. All these schools are privately run and are forced to compete with one another in order to attract buyers. A considerable amount of empirical literature on the performance of these schools in the United States exists. According to Harvard economist Caroline Hoxby, although American voucher schools (or 'charter schools', as they're known) spend less money per pupil, they yield better academic results and are far more productive. In fact, in her estimates, if every school in the United States were to experience higher levels of choice and competition, school productivity – measured in terms of academic achievement per dollar spent per pupil – could rise by as much as 28 percent.[68] Twelve further empirical studies have examined the academic outcomes of school choice participants, compared to attendants of public schools. Eleven have found that choice improves outcomes. A further six were conducted on charter schools' consequences for taxpayers. All found that these schools save money.[69] If developing nations countries seek to improve education, there is little evidence that simply pouring public money into schools will make a noticeable difference. Instead, they should look to ways to make education a competitive industry, such as by introducing voucher programs. A few have moved towards this model. In the 1990s, over 125,000 poor Colombian children were provided with voucher programs to choose what schools to go to. They were selected by lottery, so it provided researchers with an excellent experiment. The *Economist* writes approvingly of this initiative:

> The subsequent results show that the children who received vouchers were 15–20 percent more likely to finish secondary education, five percentage points less likely to repeat a grade, scored a bit better on scholastic tests and were much more likely to take college entrance exams.[70]

The private sector already plays an important role in the education systems of developing economies. In Lagos, private schools account for an estimated 57 percent of all school enrolment, and surveys of slums in Kenya came up with an estimate of 44 percent.[71] India offers a particularly large-scale experiment of private education. Over half of all students are privately educated; most of them are not from wealthy families. In fact, around 70 percent of the schools charge less than 1000 rupees a month.[72] There is evidence that private schools are becoming more popular because of the apparent incompetence of government schools. A 2008 study of rural India found that private schools are the most common in areas where teacher absenteeism in government ones is the highest and operate much more efficiently than public schools (the research also found that private schools are more popular in *poorer* Indian states).[73] Some estimates show that 80 percent of these schools charge fees that are lower than the cost per pupil in public sector schools. A key reason for this is labour costs are lower; in the public sector, teachers' wages are set artificially high, according to union bargaining and political lobbying, but at the expense of the quality of children's education. This is much less the case in the private sector, where teachers' wages are determined by the market.[74] In fact, the study of rural India mentioned earlier says the following:

> Private-school teacher salaries are typically one-fifth the salary of regular public- school teachers (and are often as low as one-tenth of these salaries). This enables the private schools to hire more teachers, have lower pupil teacher ratios, and reduce multi-grade teaching... They are 2-8 percentage points less absent than teachers in public schools and 6-9 percentage points more likely to be engaged in teaching activity at any given point in time... Children in private school have higher attendance rates and superior test score performance, with the latter being true even after controlling for observed family and school characteristics.

A large segment of the globally poor population is heavily invested in private education already. However, to improve government schools, they must be forced to compete in a simulated market environment; all public funding of those schools should be replaced with a voucher-system. Ultimately, it could mean less funding for education in the long-run, as schools will become more efficient and require less money to begin with. At the same time, school quality will improve significantly as government schools learn to operate like private businesses.

Healthcare

Global private sector healthcare is widely criticised and regularly accused of neglecting the medical needs of the developing world. Such accusations are exaggerated: in total, developing countries have large purchasing power, which companies are keen to tap into. It was mentioned earlier on that Merck and Pfizer are in intense competition in producing pneumococcal vaccines, whose biggest buyers tend to be consumers in developing markets. Besides, evidence suggests that strict patent regulations bear much of the blame or high prices and undersupply.[75]

The fight against malaria also proves this point. Long-lasting insecticidal nets (LLINs) display strong effectiveness against the spread of malaria. LLIN prices have been significantly reduced in recent years – from $5 in 2014 to $2 in 2019. International charities and aid agencies have played a strong role in this price reduction, as well as in the current distribution of malaria nets, according to a UNICEF report. However, market forces have also been important in this. For example, from 2010 to 2012, the number LLIN suppliers to UNICEF rose from 7 to 11. From 2010–2011, UNICEF launched a program to increase price transparency in LLIN markets, which enhanced competition.[76]

Aid funding supports private companies manufacturing LLINs: production costs are subsidised, but other costs, such as delivery costs, are borne by manufacturers. Throughout Africa, where most malaria deaths occur, LLIN manufacturers are in fierce competition with one another, especially with predominantly Asian manufacturers. One of the biggest companies, A to Z, fills about a sixth of the demand in Sub-Saharan Africa. It only began to manufacture LLINs thanks to a corporate social responsibility partnership with Sumitomo Chemicals.[77]

It is not unreasonable to support greater international efforts to distribute LLINs in developing nations. However, a far more effective solution to the global malaria crisis arguably exists – which does not require as much international funding. This is dichloro-diphenyl-trichloroethane (DDT), which used to be (and in some places, still is) a valuable weapon against malaria. In fact, it used to be the standard preventative cure against the disease. And it worked: annual malaria deaths declined from almost a million in the 1940s to just 1500 by 1966. In 1970s, however, this tremendous decline in malaria deaths would be reversed for decades to come. Marine biologist and conservationist Rachel Carson published *Silent Spring* which purported to demonstrate that DDT had detrimental impacts on wildlife and possessed carcinogenic properties. With no replication of her findings having taken place, this prompted environmental agencies to lobby for restrictions on DDT. This brought with it the revenge of malaria. In 1990, malaria deaths had risen to 637,000. There have been some low-profile attempts to repopularise DDT.[78] A private-sector initiative in Zambia sprayed several villages with the insecticide, and consistently cut malaria deaths in half – yet prominent aid bureaucracies refuse to allow what should be an incredibly effective drug against malaria.[79] This should indicate that private companies are better disposed to make efficient and practical decisions that bureaucratic planners.

The power of competition to improve quality and cut costs in healthcare markets should not be underestimated. An OECD study (mentioned earlier in Chapter 3) found that antitrust and price transparency regulations substantially lowered healthcare and pharmaceutical prices in Guatemala, Nicaragua, and South Africa, where costs declined by at least 27 percent because of them.[80] Entrepreneurial innovativeness is certainly showing up in the hospital industry. For example, Devi Shetty is an Indian doctor who set up the Narayana Hrudayalaya hospital in 2001 which has been able to offer low-cost heart surgeries with 1000 beds in the facility. To put this into perspective, in the United States the number of beds in hospitals performing heart surgery averages at 160. This enabled the hospital to perform many heart surgeries each day, lowering costs substantially as a result. In his own words, Shetty aims for the 'Walmartisation' of Indian healthcare, to cut costs through innovation.[81] In fact, a study of the Indian state of Madhya Pradesh found that private providers tend to make a greater effort at giving patients correct diagnoses and treatments for conditions and illnesses. The authors of the study suggest that the differences in quality between private and public healthcare providers can explain the dominance of private providers in the market.[82]

The United States is typically the bogeyman of privatised healthcare, where costs are high. However, the US has managed to engineer a highly monopolised and uncompetitive healthcare market, as with pharmaceutical companies. For example, the American Medical Association (AMA) is a big union of doctors which heavily regulates the licensing of doctors. To keep doctors' wages high, they make it deliberately difficult to become a doctor in the United States.[83] It doesn't come as a surprise that America has one of the lowest number of physicians per 1000 people in the OECD.[84] This increases hospitals' labour costs, which is passed down onto consumers. Similarly, price transparency in healthcare markets is weak, which further dampens competition. If emerging countries ever want to pursue private, insurance-based healthcare models, how the United States has fared ought not to put them off: monopolies installed very much by government regulation keep insurance costs high. In fact, studies have shown that legislation of the

1980s and 1990s which largely increased the competitiveness of the insurance market contributed massively to the reduction in medical costs, yet with the continued improvement of health outcomes.[85] Despite high costs, a rarely mentioned advantage of the US healthcare system is the outcomes it produces: shorter waiting times, higher cancer survival rates, and better medical technology available than most (though not all) European healthcare systems.[86]

To make medicine and healthcare available in developing nations, aid agencies and charities could work together support and incentivise private companies. This will allow the benefits of efficiency and competitiveness to operate, while ensuring that costs are kept as low as possible. Research finds that a vouchers program, like what has been proposed in the case of education, could work well in the healthcare sector. As one study says, not only are the benefits of equity conveyed, but such a program "also provides incentives for efficiency and provider choice by involving the private sector."[87] Furthermore, a review of thirteen voucher programs in Bangladesh, Cambodia, China, Kenya, Korea, India, Indonesia, Nicaragua, Taiwan, and Uganda found that they all improved health outcomes. A vouchers program in healthcare, just like in education, would promote equity, affordability, and efficiency all at once.[88]

Another creative policy for public sector restructuring developing nations could pursue is fiscal decentralisation. Instead of complete control by the central, national government, local governments are given more autonomy over how tax rates are set, and how tax revenues are spent. A main advantage is that local governments are likely to spend money more efficiently and will be more responsive to local economic problems. This was the main finding of a study by the IMF/OECD (although the paper introduced numerous caveats: decentralisation must occur under certain political conditions, must be taken to a sufficient degree, and decentralisation of government spending must be accompanied by a decentralisation of tax revenues).[89] Certainly, fiscal decentralisation has been shown to boost growth in rich, OECD countries. But what about in less developed ones? A study from China found that decentralisation reforms significantly boosted the economic growth rates of local communities, for two reasons: local governments taxed businesses less and invested more in infrastructure.[90] It is likely that had they been carried out by national bureaucrats, these projects would have been implemented much less efficiently, weakening their economic benefits. A study of Vietnamese provinces found that decentralisation exerts similarly positive effects on growth.[91]

Eben Macdonald

CHAPTER 9

The Macroeconomics of Poverty Alleviation: Debt, Borrowing, Inflation, and Growth

The aim of this chapter is to interrogate the view that high levels of public spending are always the best ways to stimulate growth and alleviate poverty. Much literature cited in the previous chapter finds that spending can only positively impact economic growth if nations have favourable macroeconomic conditions – if debt, deficits, and inflation are relatively low. However, excessive government spending can induce destabilising macroeconomic conditions, and therefore fail to accomplish the growth-boosting, poverty-alleviating objectives it aims for.

Preventing economic instability is as essential to developing a coherent solution to global poverty as promoting economic growth is. If bad enough, recessions can have crippling effects on living standards which can be felt for decades: the Great Depression threw millions of Americans below the poverty line and the 1997 Asian financial crisis caused poverty to rise and wages to fall across the region. Historically, quite a few developing countries have been hit hard by inflationary busts: Chile, Mexico, Venezuela, Zimbabwe, Nigeria, Russia, Estonia, and Romania, to name only a handful.[1]

The Need for Freedom

If raising taxes is not sufficient, as is typically the case, governments resort to borrowing large amounts of money to pay for politically attractive public investment programs. In the previous chapter, you heard from the Congressional Budget Office about the side effects of government deficit spending – any increases in deficit-financed government spending will reduce private investment, which will either dampen or completely negate the positive impacts on growth government spending has. This explains why, beyond a certain point, debt can have a seriously negative effect on growth. A study by the Bank for International Settlements analysed a large handful of OECD countries and concluded that when government debt exceeds 85 percent of GDP, the effect becomes negative.[2] Another study, published by Harvard University, examined 44 countries over a 200-year period, and found the threshold to be 90 percent, beyond which, growth can be reduced by a whole percent. This relationship exists in both rich and emerging countries.[3] Finally, an analysis of 52 African countries over more than half a century discovered an 'inverted U' relationship between debt levels and growth: meaning, initially, higher levels of spending may genuinely serve as useful economic stimuli. However, this does not last for long, and soon debt exerts a negative force upon growth.[4]

Academic research also confirms a relationship between debt and inflation, which will be discussed in more detail in this chapter. In 2009, economist Goohoon Kwon published findings that in already highly indebted emerging economies, the relationship between additional debt and inflation is strong.[5] A later study using similar methodology and analysing 52 countries over 49 years, came to similar results.[6] According to the Harvard study mentioned previously, emerging countries with debt above the 90 percent of GDP threshold suffered inflation as much as 4 percent points higher than those with debt below 30 percent.

Attempts to alleviate poverty by spending large amounts of public money may make the situation worse, if inflation is induced, which impacts the incomes of the poor the most.

How should emerging economies respond to recessions? In truth, there really is no answer – every recession is different from the other and require different tools to fix them. If aggregate demand has fallen, and thus inflation is weak or negative, there is absolutely a need to pump stimulus capital into the economy. America's attachment to the Gold Standard during the Depression meant that the money supply could not increase, to compensate for the reduction in aggregate demand, and the severe deflation which ensued set off a destructive cycle, where capital expenditure declined, costing jobs, which reduced demand even further.[7] During deflationary recessions, large-scale government stimulus has often been very useful – such as during the 2008 Financial Crisis, especially in Australia, where a recession was virtually avoided thanks to direct cheques sent to every household in the country.[8] However, if the recession is inflationary, pumping additional spending into the economy – and thus expanding the money supply – may risk exacerbating the situation. Governments should approach recessions with even further caution if the debt is already high. As mentioned, the moment the national debt exceeds a certain threshold, growth rates sharply decline.

Inflationary recessions are typically the result of central banks expanding the money supply in the first place, for the sake of financing large scale government programs. Since they cannot be remedied by additional government spending, other means must be taken to do so. These include raising interest rates to stamp out demand for loans, liquidity, and deposits, to take pressure off prices. As is unsurprising, this induces wider negative economic effects. The risk of inflationary recessions occurring because of unbridled spending should cast doubt on the effectiveness of public sector investment in alleviating poverty. This is illustrated all too well by Latin America's history. In the 1960s, Latin American countries were accustomed to high levels of private savings and low budget deficits. However, large public social programs came into fruition in the following decade. There is a strong case to be made that they helped alleviate a variety of social problems, which improved considerably during the decade (although, it must be noted, some of those social indicators correlated strongly with GDP per capita even back then). On the other hand, economist Guy Pfeffermann explained the noticeable impacts these policies had on the favourable macroeconomic conditions of Latin America during the 1960s:

> Massive external borrowing during the 1970s... changed all that (high savings rate, low deficits). Governments and public opinion became gradually accustomed to higher public deficits, as stepped-up spending was financed largely out of foreign savings. Public savings declined and, in some cases, even became negative (as current spending and not only public investment was financed out of borrowed funds). Indeed, even some major revenue earning public utilities... which had always run operating surpluses... became net dis-savers... The public became used to double-digit inflation, which averaged at 32 percent, and exchange rates became increasingly overvalued.

This crisis continued into the 1980s. Due to even higher deficits, private borrowers were faced with crushing interest rates, and private investment was 'crowded out'. As a result, the limited data which is available suggests that Latin American poverty did not decline impressively during the 70s, despite enormous social investment. In 1980 the poverty rate of all Latin American countries was 35 percent, down from 40 percent a decade earlier.[9]

A 1991 study, co-authored William Easterly, blamed poor economic performance in a handful of South and Latin American and African countries during the 1980s on high deficits and levels of debt.[10]

Debt crises certainly don't just afflict emerging economies. Stronger and more developed economies can sleepwalk into them too. Greece, for example, learnt this the hard way, and has been plagued with a decade of persistently negative growth and double-digit unemployment.[11]

All this should send around a clear message: there can be huge risks in trying to stimulate growth and reduce poverty through large, politically attractive spending programs, if macroeconomic conditions take a turn for the worst. In fact, for governments to save money, instead of spending it recklessly, is associated with higher levels of growth. In a 1997 study, Jeffrey Sachs and Andrew Warner found that savings by national governments can have a strongly positive effect on growth – which, in their words, will "promote capital accumulation." According to their research, a 1 percent increase in government savings relative to GDP is associated with a 0.12 increase in the annual growth rate.[12] To keep growth stable, emerging economies must resist the temptation to spend lavishly.

Macroeconomic stabilisation has been a big part of South Africa's post-apartheid economic policy. In 1994, the economy was ravaged by debt, inflation, and immensely wasteful public expenditures via inefficient state-run enterprises. Since then, debt reduction and fiscal consolidation have been top priorities. These policies, alongside considerable trade and financial liberalisations have been reflected in large-scale improvements in South Africa's economic conditions, in the forms of strong income and employment growth.[13]

If debts ever need to be suddenly reduced, there are basically two policy options – spending cuts or taxes increases (or a combination of both). The important question is which is *less economically damaging*? Any Keynesian economist will tell you, it's the tax increases. But this is at odds with some of the empirical literature. A study analysed a group of OECD countries over a 30-year period, taking advantage of the IMF's record of 'fiscal adjustments', where governments have had to respond to cripplingly high debt and deficits. The study found that spending-cut-based responses to crises either produce no discernible negative economic impacts or are only 'mildly recessionary', compared to tax-increasing-based responses, which can produce substantially negative economic impacts.[14]

Macroeconomic stability is more than essential to cultivating prosperity. Destroying it through reckless public spending will bring poverty, not alleviate it.

CHAPTER 10

Multinational Enterprise: Friend or Foe to the Extremely Poor?

Western multinational corporations exploiting cheap labour in developing nations is seen as one of the greatest possible indictments of capitalism. One headline read: "$26 a month: Ethiopians are being paid world's lowest wages to make your Calvin Kleins."[1]

It is typical for Westerners to apply their First World standards to problems which afflict the globally poor, without even bothering to think from other perspectives. When in desperate poverty, people typically migrate from serene rural communities to filthy urban squalor which offends the delicate aesthetic tastes of the average Western observer. But they do such to find jobs and opportunity. It is essential that Westerners understand that. This is just as true of child labour – from our perspective, we rightly see child labour as an egregious practice. But rarely do we have the insight to admit that it has been, and still is for many people, an economic necessity. Emotionally driven, well-intentioned regulations to limit child labour have only made the situation worse.

A similar approach needs to be made to multinational sweatshop labour. As I have said repeatedly throughout this book, multinational corporations in developing countries tend to pay wages significantly higher than national averages,

The Need for Freedom

albethey still very low by our Western standards. One review collected a long list of studies corroborating this.[2] That list is displayed below:

- Affiliates of US multinational enterprises pay a wage premium that ranges from 40 percent in high-income countries to 100 percent, or double the local average, in low-income countries.
- Workers in foreign-owned and subcontracting apparel and footwear factories in Vietnam rank in the top 20 percent of the population by household expenditure.
- In Nike subcontractor factories ...annual wages were $670 compared with an average minimum wage of $134. In Indonesia, annual wages were $720 compared with an average annual minimum of $241.
- In Bangladesh, legal minimum wages in export-processing zones are 40 percent higher than the national minimum for unskilled workers, 15 percent higher for semiskilled workers, and 50 percent higher for skilled workers.
- In Mexico, firms with between 40 and 80 percent of their total sales going to exports paid wages that were, at the low end, 11 percent higher than the wages of non-export-oriented firms; for companies with export sales above 80 percent, wages were between 58 and 67 percent higher.
- In Shanghai, a survey of 48 US-based companies found that respondents paid an average hourly wage of $5.25, excluding benefits and bonuses, or about $10,900 per year. At a jointly owned GM factory in Shanghai, workers earned $4.59 an hour, including benefits; this is about three times higher than wages for comparable work at a non-US factory in Shanghai.
- The ILO...finds, based on worker surveys, that wages paid in ex- port-processing zones (EPZs) are higher than in the villages from which workers are typically recruited.

- The US Department of Labor...finds that footwear and apparel manufacturers in selected countries pay higher wages and offer better working conditions than those available in agriculture.
- The International Youth Foundation...surveyed three footwear and two apparel factories in Thailand and found that 72 percent regarded their wages as 'fair' and that 60 percent were able to accumulate savings.
- Bhattacharya (1998) reports that garment workers in Bangladesh earn 25 percent more than the country's average per capita income.
- Razafindrakoto and Roubaud find that EPZ workers in Madagascar earned 15 to 20 percent more than the average worker in the rest of the economy, even after controlling for education level, extent of professional experience, and tenure in employment.
- Workers in the Philippine EPZ reported themselves to be better off after finding employment in the EPZ during the 1990s. As reported by the World Bank, 47 percent of workers earned enough to have some savings, as compared to 9 percent before employment in the zone. In addition, employees received social security, medical care, paid vacation, sick leave, maternity leave, and other employee benefits.

If that's not enough, research by the economist Benjamin Powell has found that sweatshop wages in the apparel industry are up to *over 700 percent average national incomes*.[3] The OECD has also confirmed that in developing countries, multinational corporations pay better wages than their domestic counterparts.[4] Some argue that multinational corporations pay higher wages only because they tend to be concentrated in more advanced sectors of the economy. However, after controlling for this bias, studies still find that workers in multinational firms earn comparatively more than in domestic firms; based on data from Indonesia and Brazil, foreign takeover of firms is found to increase wages by between 10 and 20 percent.[5] Quite a few developing economies have strongly benefitted from the presence of multinational corporations – Vietnam and Bangladesh being two notable examples.

A possible spill-over benefit to multinational corporate presence is increasing the competitiveness of the labour market, therefore causing wages across the board to increase. Since they offer comparatively higher wages, smaller firms need to raise their own workers' wages to maintain their own workforces. Recall the Baumol effect: even when productive jobs become better paid, the same happens with less productive ones, because workers migrate from the low-wage to the high-wage jobs. This limits the supply of the low-wage workers, causing their pay to rise.

There are different reasons why multinational corporations pay such 'high' wages to workers. Understandably, these firms are more technologically advanced than domestic ones – meaning worker productivity is significantly higher. Another is that because labour demand is so high, multinational firms naturally have to raise wages relative to other firms, in order to outcompete them for labour. Arguably, the average lack of size in businesses in developing economies means there is insufficient labour demand to create jobs and raise incomes – which is why multinational presence is needed. Recall, mentioned earlier, that African businesses are 20 percent smaller than their counterparts in other locations; recall also that smaller firms tend to be less productive and provide workers with a lower standard of living. Increasing average firm size in developing economies would be a good way to increase living standards – and the presence of multinational businesses can certainly help with that.

A common perception is that developing economies are usually driven by the apparel industry. This is incorrect. In 2015, Africa's manufacturing sector was eight times larger than its size in 2000. A lot of this has been driven by foreign investment; Renault created thousands of automotive jobs by locating in Morocco and cement production is a large source of employment in many other African countries.

Manufacturing is a strong driver of economic growth, involving up to nine-tenths of all private R&D spending; and on top of that, manufacturing jobs tend to deliver better wages and working conditions.[6]

Not only does multinational investment provide developing nations with 'high-wage jobs', but the innovations which it has produced have heavily benefited those countries. Companies like Celtel in the Congos, and Safaricom in Kenya have facilitated enormous growth in Africa's telecoms market, for example.

Mobile phones have had a tremendous impact on the lives of ordinary people in dozens of poor countries. They have greatly reduced communication costs, thereby having a host of economic and social benefits, such as enabling poor farmers to contact local markets and secure deals. One survey in Tanzania found that 67 percent of farmers think that mobile phone usage increases agricultural profits, 50 percent that it decreases the cost of farming, and 47 percent that it decreases the time taken to farm.[7] A study by the School of Management and Social Sciences at Lagos, Nigeria, concluded:

> Mobile penetration and squared mobile penetration have significant positive effects on agricultural value added, implying that mobile penetration has an increasing effect on agricultural value added… Mobile phones (and internet) play significant roles in agricultural development, as agricultural development also plays important roles in the expansion of mobile phones (and internet).[8]

Another study from Tanzania even found that mobile phone usage actually contributes slightly to reducing rural poverty and raising living standards thanks to the expansion of market access[9]; a study by MIT found that increased access to M-PESA, Kenya's most popular mobile phone service, pulled

The Need for Freedom

194,000 people out of poverty. It had a noticeable gender empowerment aspect to it, helping to move 185,000 women from farms to business occupations.[10]

Unfortunately, government intrusion in the marketplace has interfered with populations gaining access to mobile phones. In Tanzania, mobile phone companies pay as much as half of their revenues to the government.[11] In Ghana, taxation inflates the price of handsets by 38 percent.[12]

In the 1990s, the seed company Monsanto invented a small package of basic seed and fertilisers, aimed specifically at low-income farmers – it was known as the Combi-Pack. This has been shown to greatly benefit low-income farmers in poor rural areas, such as by boosting crop yields, improving soil condition, and reducing input costs, especially considering that the Packs are sold at very low costs to farmers. What's more, the Combi-Pack has helped especially disadvantaged groups within Africa: thanks to apartheid-era policies, South African Blacks live on predominantly marginal lands, where soil conditions are poor. Combi-Packs have helped mitigate this and boost crop yields.

Another benefit of the Combi-Pack has been to create opportunities for young people. In Mlondozi, South Africa, unemployment can be as high as 70 percent – and those who are employed tend to be in the informal sector. Monsanto has established programs to teach farmers how to use no-till conservation farming, as well as to make use of Combi-Pack resources. So far, the program has been successful: managing to create hundreds of jobs on predominantly smallholder farms, it has also managed to greatly boost years. In fact, in 1999, the program's first year of implementation, no-till farming in Mlondozi yielded crop ton per hectare 124 percent higher than conventional farming.[13]

Multinational investment would have contributed noticeably to alleviating world hunger, if regulators had allowed such: Monsanto had been collaborating with laboratories to create golden rice, a genetically modified form of rice which contains higher levels of vitamin A. The WHO estimates that every year 2.7 million children die as a result of vitamin A deficiency, and hundreds of thousands more suffer blindness.[14] Had it been approved by regulators, golden rice could have saved millions of lives. But it never was, mostly because of the superstitious paranoia about genetically modified organisms (GMOs), which is as scientifically substantiated as the claim that vaccines cause autism. The development of golden rice was eventually suffocated by government overregulation, despite widespread proof that it was a safe food. In fact, much of the suspicion of the food came from the fact it had widespread corporate funding, and environmental groups lobbied hard for its restriction.[15] In the words of science writer Ed Regis, "[T]he effects of withholding, delaying, or retarding Golden Rice development through overcautious regulation has imposed unconscionable costs in terms of years of sight and lives lost."[16]

Foreign private investment has contributed to the expansion of tractor usage in developing nations. Tractors significantly boost agricultural productivity – and globally, a sizeable portion of farmers do not have access to them. Tractors are such vital commodities that governments do the best they can to make sure farmers have access to them, such as by importing and then selling them on at a heavily subsidised price. On paper, this sounds like a perfectly reasonable idea – until you examine its effects more closely. A study from Ghana – where this policy is in place – found that the majority of tractor owners own second-hand tractors purchased from private suppliers, not the government's program. In fact, small-scale farmers prefer to hire tractors from medium- and large-scale farms, instead of from state providers. Why? The answer lies in the issue of the government's typical incompetence and lack of entrepreneurialism. While private providers tend to import cheaper second-hand vehicles (which are more popular), the state imports brand new ones, which are significantly more expensive, even with the subsidies. What the private sector tends to offer has other considerable advantages. The second-hand vehicles have spare parts which can be sold by farmers at cheap prices and are popular in local markets. The new brands, however, have changed quite a lot, and the spare parts aren't popular for trading.[17] This case study should clearly illustrate that the public sector cannot interact with a marketplace in the same way the private sector can. Thus, it is the private sector which has filled up the demand for tractors – and bigger corporations often supply those imports. These manufacturers include Massey Ferguson, Mahindra & Mahindra, and John Deere.

None of this means that small businesses do not have an important role to play in economic development. A survey of 225 small manufacturing businesses in Tanzania found that small businesses can contribute to poverty reduction through sustaining job creation and income growth.[18] However, the presence of bigger businesses is needed to inject competition into developing labour markets and boost productivity growth.

Labelling multinational corporations 'exploitative' of developing countries is simplistic and fails to consider the advantages they may bring to subsidiary countries. These firms are noticeably more efficient than the domestic companies of the subsidiary countries, pay significantly higher wages, and energise labour markets with competition. On top of that, they have provided emerging economies with hugely beneficial innovations. In fact, to stimulate the growth of living standards in poorer countries, *greater* multinational presence is required. Since the wages they offer are so much higher, they inevitably inject competition into the labour market, which has positive spill-over effects.

Conclusion

The whole thesis of this book can be summed up as following:

1. Economic growth is the best tool for poverty reduction
2. Economic liberalism provides the greatest stimulus to economic growth
3. Therefore, economic liberalism is the best system to reduce poverty.

The growth of average income – or GDP per capita, as it is known – has been very strongly correlated with reductions in poverty and the income growth of the poorest segments of society. On top of that, economic growth has been highly correlated with improvements in health, social, and environmental indicators. As the average person gets richer, children become less likely to die before the age of five, life expectancy rises, workers have to toil away for fewer hours, young children exit the workforce to attend school, and the air becomes cleaner and less polluted. It was economic growth that enriched the West: poverty and the most extreme drudgery imaginable were ended by growth before labour unions or regulation played important roles in economic life. Considering a variety of case studies, developing economies must see that regulations can often be counterproductive and harm those they intend to help.

Policymakers hotly debate the best ways to fuel economic growth; we have considered many options. Foreign aid from developed countries is a popular way to alleviate extreme poverty. The empirical literature on this is highly mixed on the benefits of foreign aid. Some studies do suggest that it can have extraordinarily positive impacts on living standards. They're in the minority, though – but as are the ones with highly pessimistic views of aid. The most reasonable and academically credible position is that aid can increase living standards, contingent on governments focusing on good economic policies in the first place, so that spending can be absorbed productively and efficiently. Any rational policymaker will ask what those policies ought to be instead of simply asking for more aid spending.

The same is the case for domestic public spending. The truth is more complex than 'public spending is always good for growth', as the socialist left maintains, but also 'government spending is always a recipe for disaster', as the libertarian right argues. Generally, smaller governments produce higher growth rates. One of the reasons for this, conceivably, is that less government spending maximises the effectiveness of government spending. Too much of it can mean crushingly high tax rates and deficits which can hamper private enterprise and investment. Even more so, public bureaucracies shouldn't be trusted entirely with spending money, given their history of inefficiency and incompetence. Public services are best delivered through public-private partnerships: voucher programs would be ideal for education and healthcare, as they've been shown to substantially improve outcomes in both developed and non-developed countries.

Overall, the evidence finds that, far and away, economic liberalism is the best system for boosting economic growth. Most developed economies are suffocated significant regulatory barriers to business activity, impediments to free trade, as well as an absence of property rights.

Meanwhile, trade liberalisation, financial liberalisation, privatisation, corporate tax reductions, and labour market deregulation have been shown to boost growth by enabling businesses to invest and accumulate capital, with the effect of increasing labour productivity, through spurring competition. Business competition is the star of the show in every successful economy: when firms known that they have competitors, they feel the need to reduce prices and innovate heavily. They know they need to get their game together, and act as productive and efficient enterprises.

Since it boosts economic growth the most out of many manjor policy ideas, economic liberalism is the best solution to global poverty. Many developing economies have gone down its path, with spectacular results – China, India, Vietnam, Rwanda, Botswana, Uganda, Chile, Estonia, Romania, Lithuania, and Georgia. These countries were once mired in poverty and political fragmentation. They were once famous for wars, famines, great ethnic conflicts, and economic chaos. Now, they lead the world in economic growth. They've built their prosperity off openness to trade, favourable regulatory environments, strong property rights, and an acceptance of multinational business. Though affluent observers are understandably appalled by the working conditions these companies have to offer, they offer one of the best paths out of poverty for emerging economies.

Extreme levels of poverty persist across the world, affecting hundreds of millions – and the Covid crisis has made things worse. However, with the correct economic policies, this can be fixed.

References

CHAPTER 1:

1. The World Bank, *Covid-19 to Add as Many as 150 Million Extreme Poor by 2021*: https://www.worldbank.org/en/news/press-release/2020/10/07/covid-19-to-add-as-many-as-150-million-extreme-poor-by-2021

2. NEWS/ Pfizer and Biontech Announce Vaccine Candidate Against COVID-19 Achieved Success in First Interim Analysis from Phrase 3 Study, November 9, 2020: https://www.pfizer.com/news/press-release/press-release-detail/pfizer-and-biontech-announce-vaccine-candidate-against

3. OurWorldInData, Statistics and Research, *Coronavirus (Covid-19) Vaccinations*: https://ourworldindata.org/covid-vaccinations

4. Worldometer, GDP per capita: https://www.worldometers.info/gdp/gdp-per-capita/

5. John. F. Kennedy, Presidential Library and Museum, *Remarks at the University of Kansas, March 18, 1968*: https://www.jfklibrary.org/learn/about-jfk/the-kennedy-family/robert-f-kennedy/robert-f-kennedy-speeches/remarks-at-the-university-of-kansas-march-18-1968

6. Kirk Johnson and Robert Rector, *Understanding Poveryt in America*, January 5, 2004: https://www.heritage.org/welfare/report/understanding-poverty-america

7. *OurWorldInData, The share of people living in extreme poverty vs GDP per capita, 2017*: https://ourworldindata.org/grapher/the-share-of-people-living-in-extreme-poverty-vs-gdp-per-capita?xScale=linear

8. Xavier Sala-i-Martin and Maxim Pinkoviskiy, *African Poverty is Falling... Much Faster Than You Think!*, February 2010: https://www.nber.org/system/files/working_papers/w15775/w15775.pdf

9. Aart Kraay and David Dollar, *Growth is Good for the Poor*, April 2001: https://elibrary.worldbank.org/doi/pdf/10.1596/1813-9450-2587

10. OECD, *Growth and income inequality: trends and policy implications*, April 2015: https://www.oecd.org/economy/labour/Growth-and-income-inequality-trends-and-policy-implications.pdf

The Need for Freedom

11. Dollar, Kleineberg and Kraay, *Growth is Still Good for the Poor*, 2013: https://openknowledge.worldbank.org/handle/10986/16001

12. Dollar, Kleineberg and Kraay, *Growth, inequality and social welfare: Cross-country evidence*, 19 November, 2014, Vox.EU Center for Economic Policy and Research: https://voxeu.org/article/growth-inequality-and-social-welfare

13. Richard Adams, *Economic Growth, Inequality, and Poverty: Findings from a New Data Set*, 2003: https://openknowledge.worldbank.org/handle/10986/19109

14. World Bank Group, *A Measured Approach to Ending Poverty and Boosting Shared Prosperity*, 2015: https://openknowledge.worldbank.org/bitstream/handle/10986/20384/9781464803611.pdf

15. See Max Roser, Economic Growth, *OurWorldInData*: https://ourworldindata.org/economic-growth

16. See *OurWorldInData*, *Health Expenditure vs. GDP*, 2014: https://ourworldindata.org/grapher/healthcare-expenditure-vs-gdp

17. David Bloom et al., *The promise and peril of universal healthcare*, Science, August 24, 2018: https://www.science.org/doi/10.1126/science.aat9644

18. Office for National Statistics, *How has life expectancy changed over time?*, 9 September 2015: https://www.ons.gov.uk/peoplepopulationandcommunity/birthsdeathsandmarriages/lifeexpectancies/articles/howhaslifeexpectancychangedovertime/2015-09-09

19. For a more in-depth analysis of this problem, see Harry Patrinos and George Psacharopoulos *Strong link between education and earnings*, 7 December, 2017: https://blogs.worldbank.org/education/strong-link-between-education-and-earnings

20. The Environmental Kuznets Curve was first proposed by economists Gene Grossman and Alan Krueger in *Economic Growth and the Environment*, February 1994: https://www.nber.org/papers/w4634

21. Dimitrios Paraskevopoulos, *An Empirical Analysis of the Environmental Kuznets Curve Hypothesis Over Two Centuries: Evidence from the UK and US*, October 2009: https://core.ac.uk/download/pdf/292384258.pdf

22. Theodore Panayotou, *Empirical Tests and Policy Analysis of Environmental Degradation at Different Stages of Economic Development*, January 1993: https://www.ilo.org/public/libdoc/ilo/1993/93B09_31_engl.pdf

23. Matt Ridley, *The Rational Optimist* (Harper, 2010)

24. See William Baumol and William Bowen, *Performing Arts, the Economic Dilemma: a study of problems common to theatre, opera, music, and dance*, Cambridge, Mass.: M.I.T Press

25. Ravi Balakrishnan et al. *Commodity Cycles, Inequality, and Poverty in Latin America*, 26 April, 2021: https://www.imf.org/en/Publications/Departmental-Papers-Policy-Papers/Issues/2021/04/26/Commodity-Cycles-Inequality-and-Poverty-in-Latin-America-45381

CHAPTER 2:

1. See Max Roser, *Economic Growth*, *OurWorldInData*: https://ourworldindata.org/economic-growth; for statistics on life expectancy, see Max Roser, Esteban Ortiz-Ospina and Hannah Ritchie, *Life Expectancy*, *OurWorldInData*: https://ourworldindata.org/life-expectancy; for statistics on infant mortality, see Max Roser, Hannah Ritchie and Bernadeta Dadonaite, *Child and Infant Mortality*, *OurWorldInData*: https://ourworldindata.org/child-mortality

2. Max Roser (2013) - "Economic Growth". *Published online at OurWorldInData.org*. Retrieved from: 'https://ourworldindata.org/economic-growth'

3. Ian Gazeley and Andrew Newell, *The end of destitution: Evidence from British working households 1904-1937*, University of Sussex: https://www.sussex.ac.uk/webteam/gateway/file.php?name=wps-2-2010/pdf&site=24

4. Klaus Walde, Trade union density from 1880 to 2008 for selected OECD countries, Johanes Gutenberg Universitat Mainz: https://www.macro.economics.uni-mainz.de/klaus-waelde/trade-union-density-from-1880-to-2008-for-selected-oecd-countries/

5. Nominal wages, consumer prices, and real wages in the UK, United Kingdom, 1750 to 2015, *OurWorldInData*: https://ourworldindata.org/grapher/nominal-wages-consumer-prices-and-real-wages-in-the-uk-since-1750?country=~GBR

6. UVA, Miller Center, Presidential Speeches, January 8, 1964: State of the Union, Miller Center: https://millercenter.org/the-presidency/presidential-speeches/january-8-1964-state-union

7. Ann Bixby, *Public Social Welfare Expenditure, Fiscal Years 1965-87*: https://www.ssa.gov/policy/docs/ssb/v53n2/v53n2p10.pdf.
For statistics on poverty, see ASPE, Alay Chaudry et al., *Poverty in the United States: 50-Year Trends and Safety Net Impacts*, March 2016: https://aspe.hhs.gov/sites/default/files/private/pdf/154286/50YearTrends.pdf

8. Gwendolyn Mink and Alice O'Connor, *Poverty in the United States: An Encyclopaedia of History, Politics and Policy*

9. Robert Plotnick and Eugene Smolensky, *The Twentieth Century Record of Inequality and Poverty in the United States*, the Institute for Research on Poverty, July 1998: https://www.irp.wisc.edu/publications/dps/pdfs/dp116698.pdf

10. Aaron O'Neill, *Annual growth of real GDP in the United States of America from 1930 to 2020*, August 23, 2021: https://www.statista.com/statistics/996758/rea-gdp-growth-united-states-1930-2019/

11. Alan Greenspan and Adrian Wooldridge, *Capitalism in America: A History*, 2018, p. 253

12. Cecil Bohanon, *Economic Recovery: Lessons from the Post-World War II Period*, September 10, 2012: https://www.mercatus.org/publications/economic-history/economic-recovery-lessons-post-world-war-ii-period

13. Matthew Mitchell, *Federal, State, and Local Expenditures as a Share of GDP at WWII Levels*, August 29, 2011: https://www.mercatus.org/publications/government-spending/federal-state-and-local-expenditures-share-gdp-wwii-levels

14. Alan Greenspan and Adrian Wooldridge, *Capitalism in America: A History*, 2018, p. 283

15. Tax Foundation, 10 Common Tax Myths, Debunked, (see 'Myth 2: U.S. income taxes on the rich were much higher in the 1950s'): https://taxfoundation.org/10-common-tax-myths/

16. Paul Moreno, *Unions and Discrimination*, Cato Journal: https://www.cato.org/sites/cato.org/files/serials/files/cato-journal/2010/1/cj30n1-4.pdf

17. George Stigler, *The Economics of Minimum Wage Legislation,* American Economic Review, 1946

18. Leonard Thomas, *Illiberal Reformers: Race, Eugenics, and American Economics in the Progressive Era*, 2016

19. Esteban Ortiz-Ospina and Max Roser (2016) - "Child Labor". *Published online at OurWorldInData.org.* Retrieved from: 'https://ourworldindata.org/child-labor'

20. International Labour Organisation, *World Report on Child Labour: Economic vulnerability, social protection and the fight against child labour*, 2013, pp. xvi

21. *Ibid*, pp. xvi

22. Ludwig Von Mises, *Human Action* (New Haven, Connecticut: Yale Press University, 1949), p. 615

23. Prashant Bharadwaj et al., *Perverse Consequences of Well-Intended Regulations: Evidence from India's Child Labor Ban*, October 2013: https://www.nber.org/papers/w19602

24. Clark Nardinelli, *Child Labor and the Industrial Revolution* (Indiana University Press, 1990)

25. Robert Whaples, *Child Labor in the United States*, Wake Forest University: https://eh.net/?s=child+labor

26. *Ibid.*

27. Carolyn Moehling, *State Child Labor Laws and the Decline of Child Labor*, Explorations in Economic History, January 1999: https://www.sciencedirect.com/science/article/abs/pii/S0014498398907124

28. Eric Edmonds, *Child Labor*, February 2007, Figure 10. See also Sonia Bhalotra, *Child Mortality and Economic Growth*, CMPO, University of Bristol, January 2008. See also The decline of child morality by levels of prosperity, 1990 to 2019: https://ourworldindata.org/grapher/the-decline-of-child-mortality-by-level-of-prosperity-endpoints

29. Charlie Giattino, Esteban Ortiz-Ospina and Max Roser (2013) - "Working Hours". *Published online at OurWorldInData.org*. Retrieved from: 'https://ourworldindata.org/working-hours' [Online Resource]

30. Michael Huberman and Chris Minns, *The times they are not changin': Days and hours of work in Old and New Worlds, 1870-2000*, 12 July, 2007, see Table 1: https://personal.lse.ac.uk/minns/Huberman_Minns_EEH_2007.pdf

31. The Economist, *Proof that you should get a life*, 9 December, 2014: https://www.economist.com/free-exchange/2014/12/09/proof-that-you-should-get-a-life

32. Guomundur Haraldsson and Jack Kellam, *Going Public: Iceland's journey to a shorter working week*, Autonomy, June 2021: https://autonomy.work/wp-content/uploads/2021/06/ICELAND_4DW.pdf

33. Robert Whaples, *Where Is There Consensus Among American Economic Historians? The Results of a Survey on Forty Propositions?*, The Journal of Economic History, March 1995: https://www.jstor.org/stable/2123771

34. Robert Whaples, *Hours of Work in U.S. History*, Wake Forest University: https://eh.net/encyclopedia/hours-of-work-in-u-s-history/

35. Michael Buehler et al., *More than 2 million people die at work each year. Here's how to prevent it*, World Economic Forum, March 23, 2017: https://www.weforum.org/agenda/2017/03/workplace-death-health-safety-ilo-fluor/

36. Jamie Whyte, *Why workplace accidents could be good for us*, national, August 14, 2015

37. Burtom Folsom, *The Myth of the Robber Barons*, p. 55

38. Cato Institute, *Occupational Safety and Health Administration*, p. 374: https://www.cato.org/sites/cato.org/files/serials/files/cato-handbook-policymakers/1997/9/105-36.pdf

39. *Ibid.*, p. 378

40. Andreas Bergh, *The Rise, Fall and Revival of the Swedish Welfare State: What are the Policy Lessons from Sweden?*, Research Institute of Industrial Economics, 2011: https://papers.ssrn.com/sol3/papers.cfm?abstract_id=1884528

41. *Ibid.*

42. Historical Index of Economic Liberty, Espacio Investiga: https://espacioinvestiga.org/hiel-eng/hiel-global-data/hiel-comparativo-eng/?lang=en

43. For statistics on infant mortality, see Aaron O'Neill, *Infant mortality in Sweden 1800-2020*, October 16, 2019. For statistics on life expectancy, see SCB, *Life expectancy 1751-2020*, 2021

44. Jesper Roine and Daniel Waldenström, *The Evolution of Top Incomes in an Egalitarian Society; Sweden, 1903-2004*, Journal of Public Economics, November 13, 2008

45. Paul Roberts and Karen Araujo, The Capitalist Revolution in Latin America (New York: Oxford University Press, 1997), p. 149

46. Deidre McCloskey, *Bourgeoisie Dignity: Why Economics Can't Explain the Modern World* (University of Chicago Press, 2011), p. 229

47. Joel Mokyr, The British Industrial Revolution (Taylor and Francis, 1999), p. 28

48. *Ibid.*, p. 25

49. Historical Index of Economic Liberty, Espacio Investiga

50. Esteban Ortiz-Ospina and Max Roser (2016) - "Taxation". *Published online at OurWorldInData.org.* Retrieved from: 'https://ourworldindata.org/taxation' [Online Resource]

51. Esteban Ortiz-Ospina and Max Roser (2016) - "Government Spending". *Published online at OurWorldInData.org.* Retrieved from: 'https://ourworldindata.org/government-spending' [Online Resource]

CHAPTER 3:

1. Adam Smith, *An Inquiry into the Nature and Causes of the Wealth of Nations* (London: Methuen, 1904),

2. Burt Folsom, *The Myth of the Robber Barons* (Young America's Foundation, 1991)

3. Center for Disease Control and Prevention, *Pfizer-Biontech Vaccine Overview and Safety*, September 20, 2021: https://www.cdc.gov/coronavirus/2019-ncov/vaccines/different-vaccines/Pfizer-BioNTech.html

4. Sexton and Zhang, 2006

5. Marta Stryszowska, *Estimation of Loss in Consumer Surplus Resulting from Excessive Pricing of Telecommunication Services in Mexico*, OECD Digital Economy Papers, 2012: https://www.oecd.org/centrodemexico/49539257.pdf

6. Carlos Urzúa, *Distributive and Regional Effects of Monopoly Power*, Economía Mexicana NUEVA ÉPOCA, 2013: https://econpapers.repec.org/paper/egadocume/200904.htm

7. Yin-Fang Zhang et al., *Electricity Sector Reform in Developing Countries: An Econometric Assessment of the Effects of Privatisation*, Competition and Regulation, Centre on Regulation and Competition, 2008: https://econpapers.repec.org/paper/agsidpmcr/30593.htm

8. Ivaldi et al., *Competition Policy for Shared Prosperity and Inclusive Growth*, World Bank Group, 2017, chapter 3: https://openknowledge.worldbank.org/handle/10986/27527

9. Joseph DiMasi et al., The price of innovation: new estimates of drug development costs, March 2003: https://pubmed.ncbi.nlm.nih.gov/12606142/. For the other study mentioned, see Daniel Klein, *Drug-Approval Denationalization*, April 6, 2009, Econlib: https://www.econlib.org/library/Columns/y2009/Kleindrugapproval.html#footnote6

10. FDAReview.org, A Project of the Independent Institute, *Theory, Evidence and Examples of FDA Harm*: https://www.fdareview.org/issues/theory-evidence-and-examples-of-fda-harm/

11. Meagan Parrish, *In pharma, cancer is king*, pharmaManufacturing, March 23, 2020: https://www.pharmamanufacturing.com/articles/2020/in-pharma-cancer-is-king/

12. Amy Brown, *Merck and Pfizer square up for pneumococcal vaccine fight*, Evaluate Vantage, June 23, 2020: https://www.evaluate.com/vantage/articles/news/merck-and-pfizer-square-up-pneumococcal-vaccine-fight

13. Damian Hattigh et al., *Lions (still) on the move: Growth in Africa's consumer sector*, McKinsey & Company, October 2, 2017: https://www.mckinsey.com/industries/consumer-packaged-goods/our-insights/lions-still-on-the-move-growth-in-africas-consumer-sector

14. Joseph Schumpeter, Capitalism, Socialism and Democracy (Harper & Brothers, 1942),

15. William Nordhaus, *Schumpeterian Profits in the American Economy: Theory and Measurement*, April 2004: https://www.nber.org/papers/w10433

16. Ufuk Akcigit et al., *Taxation and Innovation in the 20th Century*, September 2018: https://www.nber.org/papers/w24982

17. Ludwig Von Mises, *Planning for Freedom: And Other Essays and Addresses* (Liberty Fund Inc: 1952), p. 146

18. Steve Landsburg, The Path to Prosperity, April 10, 2012: http://www.thebigquestions.com/2012/04/10/the-path-to-prosperity/

19. For data on wage growth, see *United States Wages and Salaries Growth*, Trading Economics, July 2021. For data on capital investment growth, see OECD Data, *Investment (GFCF)*.

20. Robert Hall et al., *Why Do Some Countries Produce So Much Output Per Worker Than Other Countries?*, National Bureau of Economic Research, 1998: https://www.nber.org/system/files/working_papers/w6564/w6564.pdf

21. Jon Strand, *The Relationship Between Wages and Firm Size: An Information Theoretical Analysis*, International Economic Review, February 1987: https://www.jstor.org/stable/2526859

22. Matt Bruenig, *Small Businesses are Overrated*, Jacobin, January 16, 2018: https://jacobinmag.com/2018/01/small-business-workers-wages

23. Nicholas Bloom and John Van Reenen, *Why Do Management Practises Differ Across Firms and Countries?*, Journal of Economic Perspectives, Winter 2010: https://www.aeaweb.org/articles?id=10.1257/jep.24.1.203

24. Ellora Derenoncourt et al., *Spillover Effects from Voluntary Employer Minimum Wages*, March 1, 2021: https://papers.ssrn.com/sol3/papers.cfm?abstract_id=3793677

25. José Azar et al., *Labor Market Concentration*, December 2017: https://www.nber.org/papers/w24147

26. Will Abel et al., *Monopsony in the UK*, VOX.EU Center for Economic and Policy Research, January 23, 2019: https://voxeu.org/article/monopsony-uk

27. Kevin Rinz, *Labor Market Concentration, Earnings, and Inequality*, United States Census Bureau, September 2018: https://www.census.gov/library/working-papers/2018/adrm/carra-wp-2018-10.html

28. Johnathon Haskel, *Imperfect Competition, Work Practises and Productivity Growth*, Queen Mary University of London, School of Economics and Finance, 1990: https://ideas.repec.org/p/qmw/qmwecw/222.html

29. Thomas Holmes and James Schmitz, *Competition and Productivity: A Review of the Evidence*, Federal Reserve Bank of Minneapolis, February 2010: https://core.ac.uk/reader/6247637

30. Competition and Markets Authority, *Productivity and competition: A summary of the evidence*, July 9, 2015: https://assets.publishing.service.gov.uk/government/uploads/system/uploads/attachment_data/file/909846/Productivity_and_competition_report__.pdf

31. Peter Warr, *Productivity Growth in Thailand and Indonesia: How Agriculture Contributes to Economic Growth*, Australian Agricultural and Resource Economics Society, 2006: https://ideas.repec.org/p/ags/aare06/139925.html

32. Pontus Braunerhjelm and Johan Eklund, *Taxes, Tax Administration Burdens and New Firm Formation*, Swedish Entrepreneurship Forum, 2013: https://entreprenorskapsforum.se/wp-content/uploads/2013/05/WP_23.pdf

33. Leora Klapper et al., Entry Regulations as a Barrier to Entrepreneurship, March 2004: https://www.nber.org/system/files/working_papers/w10380/w10380.pdf

34. Simeon Djankov et al., *Regulation and Growth*, Available at SSRN, March 29, 2006: https://papers.ssrn.com/sol3/papers.cfm?abstract_id=893321

35. William Crain and Nicole Craine, *The Information Technology Revolution and the Transformation of the Small Business Economy: A Collection of Essays*, p. 56

36. Business and Human Rights Resource Centre, October 2, 2018: https://www.business-humanrights.org/en/latest-news/amazon-raises-minimum-wage-for-us-uk-employees-in-victory-for-workers-pushing-for-better-pay/

37. Fabiano Schivardi et al., *Entry Barriers in Retail Trade*, February 15, 2011: https://onlinelibrary.wiley.com/doi/abs/10.1111/j.1468-0297.2009.02348.x

38. Lee Branstetter et al., *Prometheus unbound? The modest benefits of entry deregulation in Portugal*, VOX.EU Center for Economic Policy and Research, September 18, 2014: https://voxeu.org/article/prometheus-unbound-modest-benefits-entry-deregulation-portugal

39. Federico Cingano et al., *Boosting growth in high-debt times: The role of service deregulation*, VOX.EU Center for Economic Policy and Research, December 6, 2011: https://voxeu.org/article/boosting-growth-service-deregulation

40. *Competition Policy for Shared Prosperity and Inclusive Growth*, World Bank Group, p. 28-29: https://openknowledge.worldbank.org/handle/10986/27527

41. Cheng Chen and Claudia Steinwender, *Does more competition spur innovation or discourage it?*, LSE blog, March 6, 2020: https://blogs.lse.ac.uk/businessreview/2020/03/06/does-more-competition-spur-innovation-or-discourage-it/

42. Jose Larraz et al., Productivity and value added distribution in family-owned businesses, University of Lleida, December 2016: https://core.ac.uk/download/pdf/84926212.pdf

43. Nina Pavcnik, *Trade Liberalization, Exit, and Productivity Improvements; Evidence from Chilean Plants*, The Review of Economic Studies, January 1, 2002: https://academic.oup.com/restud/article-abstract/69/1/245/1584480

44. Bishwanath Goldar et al., *Trade Liberalization and Price-Cost Margin in Indian Industry*, March 6, 2007: https://onlinelibrary.wiley.com/doi/abs/10.1111/j.1746-1049.2005.tb00949.x

45. James Bessen, *Accounting for Rising Corporate Profits: Intangibles or Regulatory Rents?*, Boston University School of Law, November 9, 2016: https://papers.ssrn.com/sol3/papers.cfm?abstract_id=2778641

46. Eric Goldschein, *The Incredible Story Of How De Beers Created And Lost The Most Powerful Monopoly Ever*, Insider, December 19, 2011: https://www.businessinsider.com/history-of-de-beers-2011-12?r=US&IR=T

47. Francisco Buera et al., *Well-intended policies*, Review of Economic Dynamics, January 2013: https://www.sciencedirect.com/science/article/abs/pii/S109420251200066X

48. For a description of Nigeria's state-run steel industry, see William Easterly, The White Man's Burden, p. 45; for South Africa, see *South Africa's electricity crisis: Unplugged*, The Economist, January 3, 2015: https://www.economist.com/middle-east-and-africa/2014/12/30/unplugged; for Mexico, see Paul Roberts and Karen Araujo, *The Capitalist Revolution in Latin America*; for Mongolia, see *Mongolia Public Enterprise Review, Halfway Through Reforms*, World Bank, November 4, 1996: https://documents1.worldbank.org/curated/en/862541468774006451/pdf/multi0page.pdf

49. Shawn Regan, *Socialism is Bad for the Environment*, National Review, May 16, 2019: https://www.nationalreview.com/magazine/2019/06/03/socialism-is-bad-for-the-environment/

50. Andrew Meyer et al., *Environmental performance of state-owned and privatized Eastern European energy utilities*, Energy Economics, 2013: https://ideas.repec.org/a/eee/eneeco/v36y2013icp205-214.html

51. Susmita Dasgupta et al., *Surviving Success: Policy Reform and the Future of Industrial Pollution in China*, Available at SSRN, 1998: https://papers.ssrn.com/sol3/papers.cfm?abstract_id=43301

52. *Mexico's false messiah: Voters should curb Mexico's power-hungry president*, The Economist, May 29, 2021: https://www.economist.com/leaders/2021/05/27/voters-should-curb-mexicos-power-hungry-president?utm_campaign=the-economist-today&utm_medium=newsletter&utm_source=salesforce-marketing-cloud&utm_term=2021-05-27&utm_content=article-link-1&etear=nl_today_1

53. Zeke Hausfather, *Emissions: Analysis: Why US carbon emissions have fallen 14% since 2005*, CarbonBrief, August 15, 2017: https://www.carbonbrief.org/analysis-why-us-carbon-emissions-have-fallen-14-since-2005

54. Amir Guluzade, *The role of China's state-owned companies explained*, World Economic Forum, May 7, 2019: https://www.weforum.org/agenda/2019/05/why-chinas-state-owned-companies-still-have-a-key-role-to-play/

55. Bryan Riley, *U.S. Trade Policy Gouges American Sugar Consumers*, The Heritage Foundation, June 5, 2014: https://www.heritage.org/trade/report/us-trade-policy-gouges-american-sugar-consumers/#_ftn18

56. FY 2013: Yearly Sweetener Market Report, USDA Farm Services Agency: https://www.fsa.usda.gov/FSA/webapp?area=home&subject=ecpa&topic=dsa

57. U.S. Department of Commerce, Employment Changes in U.S. Food Manufacturing: The Impact of Sugar Prices, 2006: https://legacy.trade.gov/mas/ian/build/groups/public/@tg_ian/documents/webcontent/tg_ian_002705.pdf

58. Irving Williamson et al., The Economic Effects of Significant U.S. Import Restraints, United States International Trade Commission, December 2013: https://www.usitc.gov/publications/332/pub4440.pdf

59. Johnathon Argent et al., *Competition in Kenyan Markets and its Impact on Income and Poverty: A Case Study on Sugar and Maize*, World Bank Policy Research, April 20, 2016: https://papers.ssrn.com/sol3/papers.cfm?abstract_id=2579878

CHAPTER 4:

1. Nathan Nunn, *The Long-Term Effects of Africa's Slave Trades*, Quarterly Journal of Economics, 2008: https://scholar.harvard.edu/nunn/publications/long-term-effects-africas-slave-trades

2. For Rwanda, see Karol Boudreaux, *Land Conflict and Genocide in Rwanda*, Mercatus Center, July 11, 2009; for information on the Spanish Empire, see Paul Roberts and Karen Araujo, The Capitalist Revolution in Latin America (Oxford University Press, 1997), chapter "Latin America's statist tradition". For insight into Botswana, see Daron Acemoglu et al., An African Success Story: Botswana (In Search of Prosperity: Analytical Narratives on Economic Growth, Princeton: Princeton University Press), p. 80-119, 2003

3. Jeffrey Sachs and Andrew Warner, *Sources of Slow Growth in African Economies*, Journal of African Economies, 1997

4. The World Bank, *Doing Business, Measuring Business Regulations*, 2020: https://www.doingbusiness.org/en/rankings

5. International Labour Organization, *More than 60 percent of the world's employed population are in the informal economy*, April 30, 2018: https://www.ilo.org/global/about-the-ilo/newsroom/news/WCMS_627189/lang--en/index.htm

6. World Bank Group, *Doing Business, 2020: Comparing Business Regulations in 190 Economies*, p. 63

7. Norman Loayza et al., *The Impact of Regulation on Growth and Informality: Cross-Country Evidence*, World Bank Group, May 2005: https://documents1.worldbank.org/curated/en/212041468134383114/pdf/wps36230rev.pdf

8. Valentin Petkantchin, The tax and regulatory causes of the underground economy, Institut économique Molinari, May 2013: https://www.institutmolinari.org/IMG/pdf/note0513c_en.pdf

9. Benjamin Eifert, *Do Regulatory Reforms Stimulate Investment and Growth? Evidence from the Doing Business Data, 2003-07*, Center for Global Development, January 2009: https://www.cgdev.org/sites/default/files/1420894_file_Economic_Response_FINAL.pdf

10. Fraser Institute, *Economic Freedom of the World: 2020 Annual Report*, September 10, 2020: https://www.fraserinstitute.org/economic-freedom/map?geozone=world&page=map&year=2018

11. *Ibid.*

12. For gender equality, see Rosemarie Fike, *Impact of Economic Freedom and Women's Well-Being*, March 8, 2018: https://www.fraserinstitute.org/sites/default/files/impact-of-economic-freedom-and-womens-well-being_1.pdf; for income inequality, see *Economic Freedom of the World: 2020 Annual Report*; for tolerance towards homosexuals, see Niclas Berggren et al., *Does Economic Freedom Foster Tolerance?*, Research Institute of Industrial Economics, 2012: https://www.ifn.se/wfiles/wp/wp918.pdf

13. Milton Friedman, *Capitalism and Freedom* (University of Chicago Press, 1962)

14. Jakob de Haan et al., *Does more democracy lead to greater economic freedom? New evidence for developing countries*, European Journal of Political Economy, September 2003: https://www.sciencedirect.com/science/article/abs/pii/S0176268003000132

15. Carl Knutsen, *Democracy, Dictatorship and Protection of Property Rights*, The Journal of Development Studies, April 16, 2010: https://www.tandfonline.com/doi/full/10.1080/00220388.2010.506919?src=recsys

16. John Dawson, *Institutions, Investment, and growth: New Cross-Country and Panel Data Evidence*, Economic Inquiry, September 28, 2007: https://onlinelibrary.wiley.com/doi/abs/10.1111/j.1465-7295.1998.tb01739.x

17. Hristos Doucouliagos et al., *Democracy and Economic Growth: A Meta-Analysis*, American Journal of Political Science, January 2008: https://www.jstor.org/stable/25193797

18. Shrabani et al., *The interaction effect of economic freedom and democracy on corruption: a panel cross-country analysis*, Massey University and Griffith University, November 2009: https://www.sciencedirect.com/science/article/abs/pii/S0165176509002420

19. Legatum Institute, Global Index of Economic Openness, May 16, 2019, p. 6

20. See World Economic Forum, *Competitiveness Rankings*: http://reports.weforum.org/global-competitiveness-report-2014-2015/rankings/#indicatorId=GCI.A.02. For statistics on per capita income, see Worldometer info, GDP per Capita: https://www.worldometers.info/gdp/gdp-per-capita/

21. Bentley Coffey et al., *The Cumulative Cost of Regulation*, Mercatus Center, November 14, 2016: https://papers.ssrn.com/sol3/papers.cfm?abstract_id=2869145

22. Jeffrey Sachs et al., *Sources of Slow Growth in African Economies*, Journal of African Economies, 1997, p. 352

23. John Talbott et al., *Why Many Developing Countries Just Aren't*, The Anderson School at UCLA, December 4, 2001: https://papers.ssrn.com/sol3/papers.cfm?abstract_id=292140

24. Paul Zak, *Institutions, Property Rights, and Growth*, Recherches Économiques De Louvain, 2002: https://www.cairn.info/revue-recherches-economiques-de-louvain-2002-1-page-55.htm

25. U.K. Department for International Development, *Secure property rights and development: Economic growth and household welfare*, Property rights evidence paper, April 2014: https://assets.publishing.service.gov.uk/government/uploads/system/uploads/attachment_data/file/304551/Property-rights-evidence-paper.pdf

26. Joshua Hall et al., *Economic Freedom of the World: An Accounting of the Literature*, Contemporary Economic Policy, March 12, 2013: https://onlinelibrary.wiley.com/doi/abs/10.1111/coep.12010

27. *National Resource Abundance and Economic Growth*, Jeffrey Sachs et al., National Bureau of Economic, 1995

28. Cemil Akin et al., *The Impact of Economic Freedom Upon Economic Growth: An Application On Different Income Groups*, Asian Economic and Financial Review, 2014: http://www.aessweb.com/pdf-files/aefr-2014-4(8)-1024-1039.pdf

29. Chris Doucouliagos et al., *Economic freedom and economic growth: Does specification make a difference*, European Journal of Political Economy, March 2006: https://www.sciencedirect.com/science/article/abs/pii/S017626800500042X

30. John Dawson, *Institutions, Investment, and growth: New Cross-Country and Panel Data Evidence*, Economic Inquiry, September 28, 2007: https://onlinelibrary.wiley.com/doi/abs/10.1111/j.1465-7295.1998.tb01739.x

31. Libek, *The Importance of Economic Freedom*, 2013

32. Andreas Bergh et al., *Government Size and Growth: A Survey and Interpretation of the Evidence*, Research Institute of Industrial Economics, 2011: https://journalistsresource.org/wp-content/uploads/2011/08/Govt-Size-and-Growth.pdf

33. Dimitar Chobanov et al., *What Is The Optimum Size of Government?*, Institute for Market Economics, August 2009: https://ime.bg/uploads/69a09c_OptimalSizeOfGovernment.pdf

34. Indermit Gill et al., *Golden growth: restoring the luster of the European economic model*, World Bank Group, 2012, p. 364: https://documents1.worldbank.org/curated/en/539371468036253854/pdf/Main-report.pdf

35. Jean-Pierre Chauffour, On the Relevance of Freedom and Entitlement in Development: New Empirical Evidence (1975-2007), The World Bank, May 2011: https://documents1.worldbank.org/curated/en/953181468146054735/pdf/WPS5660.pdf

36. Jamie Pavlik et al., *Economic Freedom and the Economic Consequences of the 1918 Pandemic*, May 22, 2020: https://papers.ssrn.com/sol3/papers.cfm?abstract_id=3608178

37. Richard Cebula et al., The Impact of Economic Freedom on Per Capita Real GDP: A Study of OECD Nations, 2013: https://uh.edu/~bsorense/CebulClarkMixon.pdf

38. Richard Cebula et al., *Impact of Economic Freedom, Regulatory Quality, and Taxation on the Per Capita Real Income: An Analysis for OECD Nations and Non-G8 OECD Nations*, 2014: https://www.semanticscholar.org/paper/Impact-of-Economic-Freedom%2C-Regulatory-Quality%2C-and-Cebula-Clark/b102fd28005241b918f9a7e2aaed752c5ce538a7

39. Justin Callais et al., *Economic Freedom Promotes Upward Income Mobility*, Fraser Institute, August 31, 2021: https://www.fraserinstitute.org/studies/economic-freedom-promotes-upward-income-mobility

40. Christopher Boudreaux, *Jumping off of the Great Gatsby Curve: How Institutions Facilitate Entrepreneurship and Intergenerational Mobility*, Journal of Instiutional Economics, 2014: https://home.fau.edu/cboudreaux/web/Jumping%20off%20of%20the%20Great%20Gatsby%20Curve%20pre%20print.pdf

41. Jac Heckelman, Economic Freedom and Economic Growth: A Short-Run Causal Investigation, Journal of Applied Economics, May 2000: https://ucema.edu.ar/publicaciones/download/volume3/heckelman.pdf

CHAPTER 5

1. Abebie Selassie, *Keynote Speech at the Oxford Africa Conference 2021*, IMF, May 28, 2021: https://www.imf.org/en/News/Articles/2021/05/28/sp052821-remarks-by-abebe-aemro-selassie-at-the-oxford-africa-conference-2021

2. The Legatum Institute, Global Index of Economic Openness, May 2019, p. 26

3. Davide Fuceri et al., *The Macroeconomy After Tariffs*, U.C. Berkeley, November 18, 2020: http://faculty.haas.berkeley.edu/arose/Tariffs.pdf

4. Antoine Bouët et al., *US Trade Wars with Emerging Countries in the 21st Century: Make America and its Partners Loose Again*, International Food Policy Research Institute, August 2017: https://www.parisschoolofeconomics.eu/docs/koenig-pamina/article_us_tradewars_bouet_laborde_2017.pdf

5. Arnaud Costinot, Trade Theory with Numbers: Quantifying the Consequences of Globalization, Massachusetts Institute of Technology, 2013: https://economics.mit.edu/files/9960

6. Romain Wacziarg, *Trade Liberalization and Growth: New Evidence*, World Bank Economic Review, May 2008: https://elibrary.worldbank.org/doi/abs/10.1093/wber/lhn007

7. IMF Staff, *Globe Trade Liberalization and the Developing World*, International Monetary Fund, November 2001: https://www.imf.org/external/np/exr/ib/2001/110801.htm

8. Matthias Busse et al., Trade and economic growth: A re-examination of the empirical evidence, Hamburg Institute of International Economics, February 24, 2012: https://www.econstor.eu/bitstream/10419/57921/1/715302949.pdf

9. Jeffrey Frankel et al., *Does Trade Cause Growth?*, The American Economic Review, 1999: https://www.jstor.org/stable/117025

10. The Economist, *The Corn Laws at 175: An anniversary for free traders*, June 26, 2021: https://www.economist.com/finance-and-economics/2021/06/24/an-anniversary-for-free-traders

11. Lucian Cernat et al., *Consumer benefits from EU trade liberalisation: How much did we save since the Uruguay Round*, Chief Economist Note, February 2018: https://trade.ec.europa.eu/doclib/docs/2018/february/tradoc_156619.pdf

12. Pablo Fajgelbaum, *Measuring the Unequal Benefits from Trade*, The Quarterly Journal of Economics, July 2014: https://www.nber.org/system/files/working_papers/w20331/w20331.pdf

13. Daniel Trefler, *The Long and Short of the Canada-U.S. Free Trade Agreement*, American Economic Review, September 2004: https://www.aeaweb.org/articles?id=10.1257/0002828042002633

14. Chris Edmond et al., *Competition, Markups, and the Gains from International Trade*, American Economic Review, October 2015: https://www.aeaweb.org/articles?id=10.1257/aer.20120549

15. Gary Becker, *The Economics of Discrimination* (The University of Chicago Press, 1957)

16. Sandra Black et al., *Importing Equality? The Impact of Globalisation on Gender Discrimination*, ILR Review, July 2004: https://www.jstor.org/stable/4126682

17. Ernesto Aguayo-Tellez et al., *Did Trade Liberalization Help Women? The Case of Mexico in the 1990s*, New Analyses of Worker Well-Being, 2010: https://voxeu.org/article/does-trade-liberalisation-empower-women-evidence-1990s-mexico

18. World Trade Organisation and World Bank Group, *Women and Trade: The Role of Trade in Promoting Gender Equality*, 2020, p. 4: https://www.wto.org/english/res_e/booksp_e/women_trade_pub2807_e.pdf

19. Federica Coelli et al., *Better, faster, stronger: How trade liberalisation fosters global innovation*, VoxEU CEPR, November 21, 2016: https://voxeu.org/article/how-trade-liberalisation-fosters-global-innovation

20. Nicholas Bloom et al., *Trade Induced Technical Change? The Impact of Chinese Imports on Innovation, IT and Productivity*, The Review of Economic Studies, September 17, 2015: https://academic.oup.com/restud/article-abstract/83/1/87/2461318?redirectedFrom=fulltext

21. Inmaculada Martínez-Zarzoso et al., Trade agreements and international technology transfer, August 2020: https://www.econstor.eu/bitstream/10419/223028/1/172758225X.pdf

22. Steven Matusz et al., *Adjusting to Trade Policy Reform*, The World Bank, July 1999: https://documents1.worldbank.org/curated/en/200351468741304643/pdf/multi-page.pdf

23. Pushan Insead et al., *International Trade and Unemployment: Theory and Cross-National Evidence*, Journal of International Economics, January 2009: https://www.insead.edu/sites/default/files/assets/faculty-personal-site/pushan-dutt/documents/unemployment.pdf

24. Giray Gozgor, *The Impact of Globalization on the Structural Unemployment: An Empirical Reappraisal*, International Economic Journal, December 3, 2017: https://www.tandfonline.com/doi/abs/10.1080/10168737.2017.1408666?journalCode=riej20

25. IMF Policy Paper, *Sustaining Long-Run Growth and Macroeconomic Stability in Low-Income Countries – The Role of Structural Transformation and Diversification*, International Monetary Fund, March 5, 2014: https://www.imf.org/external/np/pp/eng/2014/030514.pdf

26. Devashish Mitra, *Trade liberalization and poverty reduction*, IZA World of Labour, 2016: https://www.econstor.eu/handle/10419/148497

27. Robert King et al., *Finance and Growth: Schumpeter Might be Right*, The Quarterly Journal of Economics, August 1, 1993: https://academic.oup.com/qje/article-abstract/108/3/717/1881857

28. Patrick Hanohan, *Financial Development, Growth, and Poverty: How Close are the Links?*, World Bank Group, 2004: https://openknowledge.worldbank.org/handle/10986/14439

29. M. Hassan et al., *A Reexamination of McKinnon-Shaw Hypotheses: Evidence from Five South Asian Countries*, The Bangladesh Development Studies, December 1993: https://www.jstor.org/stable/40795490

30. Gordon Asamoah et al., *The Impact Of The Financial Sector Reforms On Savings, Investments and Growth Of Gross Domestic Product (GDP) In Ghana*, International Business & Economics Research Journal, October 2008: https://clutejournals.com/index.php/IBER/article/view/3302/3350

31. Karim Banam, *Impact of Financial Liberalization on Economic Growth in Iran: An Empirical Investigation*, June 2010: http://i-rep.emu.edu.tr:8080/xmlui/bitstream/handle/11129/687/Banam.pdf?sequence=1

32. Meghana Ayyagari et al., *Finance and Poverty: Evidence from India*, Centre for Economic Policy Discussion, June 2013: https://voxeu.org/sites/default/files/file/DP9497.pdf

33. Xavier Gine et al., *Evaluation of Financial Liberalization: A General Equilibrium Model with Constrained Occupation Choice*, World Bank Group, April 2003: https://elibrary.worldbank.org/doi/abs/10.1596/1813-9450-3014

34. World Bank Group, *A Measured Approach to Ending Poverty and Boosting Shared Prosperity*, 2015: https://openknowledge.worldbank.org/bitstream/handle/10986/20384/9781464803611.pdf

35. Thorsten Beck et al., *Big Bad Banks? The Winners and Losers from Banking Deregulation in the United States*, The Journal of Finance, September 21, 2010: https://onlinelibrary.wiley.com/doi/abs/10.1111/j.1540-6261.2010.01589.x

36. Geert Bakaert et al., *Does financial liberalization spur growth?*, Journal of Financial Economics, January 20, 2005: https://www0.gsb.columbia.edu/faculty/gbekaert/papers/financial_liberalization.pdf

37. *Big Bad Banks? The Winners and Losers from Bank Deregulation in the United States,* Thorsten Beck et al., The Journal of Finance, 2010

38. Muhammed Dandume et al., *Does Financial Liberalization Spur Economic Growth and Poverty Reduction in Six Sub-Saharan African Countries; Panel Unit Root and Panel Vector Error Correction Tests*, Munich Personal RePEc Archive, February 2014: https://mpra.ub.uni-muenchen.de/52419/1/MPRA_paper_52419.pdf

39. Thorsten Beck et al., *Banking Services for Everyone? Barriers to Banking Access and Use Around the World*, The World Bank Economic Review, October 2006: https://www.efmaefm.org/0EFMAMEETINGS/EFMA%20ANNUAL%20MEETINGS/2007-Austria/papers/0287.pdf

40. Norbert Michel, *The Case Against Dodd-Frank: How the 'Consumer Protection' Law Endangers Americans*, The Heritage Foundation, 2016, p. 12: http://thf-reports.s3.amazonaws.com/2016/The%20Case%20Against%20Dodd-Frank.pdf

41. Giovanni Cardillo et al., *Public Bailouts, Bank's Risk and Spillover Effect: The case of European banks*, European Financial Management Association, June 2018: https://www.efmaefm.org/0EFMAMEETINGS/EFMA%20ANNUAL%20MEETINGS/2018-Milan/papers/EFMA2018_0508_fullpaper.pdf

42. Allen Berger et al., Do Bank Bailouts Reduce or Increase Systemic Risk? The Effects of TARP on Financial System Stability, Journal of Financial Intermediation, June 2017: https://sc.edu/study/colleges_schools/moore/documents/finance/berger/bailouts_systemic-risk_2017-06-12_final.pdf

43. Clement Moyo et al., *Financial liberalisation, financial development and financial crises in SADC countries*, Journal of Financial Economic Policy, 2009: https://www.emerald.com/insight/publication/issn/1757-6385

44. John Boyd et al., *The Theory of Bank Risk Taking and Competition Revisited*, The Journal of Finance, May 3, 2005: https://onlinelibrary.wiley.com/doi/abs/10.1111/j.1540-6261.2005.00763.x

45. Ray Barrel et al., *Interest rate liberalization and capital adequacy in models of financial crises*, Journal of Financial Stability, December 2017: https://www.sciencedirect.com/science/article/abs/pii/S1572308916300948

46. Randal O'Toole, *How Urban Planners Caused the Housing Bubble*, Cato Institute, October 1, 2009: https://www.cato.org/sites/cato.org/files/pubs/pdf/pa646.pdf

47. Paul Roberts and Karen Araujo, The Capitalist Revolution in Latin America (New York: Oxford University Press, 1997)

48. The World Bank, *Mongolia Public Enterprise Review, Halfway Through Reforms*, November 4, 1996

49. Milton Friedman, *Free to Choose* (Harcourt, 1980), p. 1

50. Panayotis Kapopoulos et al., *Does corporate ownership structure matter for economic growth? A cross-country analysis*, Managerial and Decision Economics, October 16, 2008: https://onlinelibrary.wiley.com/doi/10.1002/mde.1442

51. Stuart Holder, *Regulation, Competition and Privatisation*, OECD, September 17-18, 1998: https://www.oecd.org/daf/ca/corporategovernanceofstate-ownedenterprises/1929658.pdf

52. Michael Wise et al., *Product Market Competition in the OECD Countries: Taking Stock and Moving Forward*, OECD Economics Department Working Papers, 2007: https://econpapers.repec.org/paper/oececoaaa/575-en.htm

53. Alberto Chong et al., *Privatization in Mexico*, Inter-American Development Bank, August 2004: https://core.ac.uk/download/pdf/6441708.pdf

54. Ahmed Galal et al., *Welfare consequences of selling public enterprises. An empirical analysis: a summary*, World Bank Group, August 1994: https://elibrary.worldbank.org/doi/pdf/10.1596/0-8213-2976-6

55. Sebastian Galiani et al., *Water for Life: The Impact of Privatization of Water Services on Child Mortality*, Journal of Political Economy, February 2005: https://www.jstor.org/stable/10.1086/426041?seq=1

56. David Arnold, *How privatisation impacts workers: Evidence from Brazil*, VOXeu CEPR, July 19, 2019: https://voxeu.org/article/how-privatisation-impacts-workers

57. Sunita Kikeri et al., Privatization in Competitive Sectors: The Record to Date, World Bank Group, June 2002, p. 17: https://openknowledge.worldbank.org/bitstream/handle/10986/14257/multi0page.pdf?sequence=1&isAllowed=y

58. David Brown et al., *Employment and Wage Effects of Privatization: Evidence from Hungary, Romania, Russia, and Ukraine*, The Economic Journal, August 6, 2009: https://academic.oup.com/ej/article-abstract/120/545/683/5089688?redirectedFrom=fulltext; David Brown et al., *Wages, Layoffs and Privatization: Evidence from Ukraine*, Journal of Comparative Economics, June 2006: https://papers.ssrn.com/sol3/papers.cfm?abstract_id=886283

59. Amir Guluzade, *The role of China's state-owned companies explained*, World Economic Forum, May 7, 2019

60. See (https://core.ac.uk/download/pdf/6341591.pdf)

61. Juliet D'Souza, Determinants of Firm Performance Improvements in Privatized Firms: The Role of Restructuring and Corporate Governance, Risk Governance and Control: Financial Markets and Institutions: https://citeseerx.ist.psu.edu/viewdoc/download?doi=10.1.1.198.9347&rep=rep1&type=pdf

62. *Ibid.*

63. John Earle, *Mass privatisation and mortality: Is job loss the link?*, VOXeu CEPR, March 7, 2009: https://voxeu.org/article/did-post-communist-privatisation-kill-not-through-job-cuts

64. Patrick Plane, Privatization and economic growth: an empirical investigation from a large sample of developing market economies, Applied Economics, October 2010: https://www.tandfonline.com/doi/abs/10.1080/000368497327245

65. Steven Barnett, *Evidence on the Fiscal and Macroeconomic Impacts of Privatization*, IMF Working Papers, July 2000: https://papers.ssrn.com/sol3/papers.cfm?abstract_id=879900

66. Leonardo Baccini et al., *Globalisation and state capitalism: Assessing the effects of Vietnam's WTO entry*, Centre for Economic Research Policy, 17 May 2019: https://voxeu.org/article/globalisation-and-state-capitalism

67. Bert Brys et al., *Taxation and Economic Growth*, OECD Economics Department Working Papers, July 3, 2008: https://www.oecd-ilibrary.org/economics/taxation-and-economic-growth_241216205486

68. Maksim Belitski et al., *Taxes, corruption, and entry*, Small Business Economics, March 23, 2016: https://link.springer.com/article/10.1007/s11187-016-9724-y

69. Rudi Rocha et al., *Do lower taxes reduce informality? Evidence from Brazil*, Journal of Development Economics, 2018: https://ideas.repec.org/a/eee/deveco/v134y2018icp28-49.html

70. R. Alison Felix, Passing the Burden: Corporate Tax Incidence in Open Economies, October 2007: https://www.kansascityfed.org/documents/118/regionalrwp-rrwp07-01.pdf

71. Kevin Hasset et al., *Taxes and Wages*, American Enterprise Institute for Public Policy Research, June 2006: https://www.aei.org/wp-content/uploads/2011/10/20060706_TaxesandWages.pdf

72. *Ibid.*

73. Mihir Desai, *Labor and Capital Shares of the Corporate Tax Burden: International Evidence*, December 2007: http://piketty.pse.ens.fr/files/Desaietal2007.pdf

74. Nida Abdioglu et al., The Effect of Corporate Tax Rate on Foreign Direct Investment: A Panel Study for OECD Countries, EGE Academic Review, June 7, 2019, p. 600: https://papers.ssrn.com/sol3/papers.cfm?abstract_id=3392359

75. *Ibid*, p. 600

76. Scott Baker et al., Corporate Taxes and Retail Prices, April 2020: https://www.nber.org/papers/w27058

77. Athiphat Muthitacharoen et al., *Location choice and tax responsiveness of foreign multinationals: Evidence from ASEAN countries*, 2018: https://econpapers.repec.org/paper/puidpaper/95.htm

78. McKinsey Global Institute, *Lions on the Move II: Realising the Potential of Africa's Economies*, September 2016, p. 76: https://www.mckinsey.com/~/media/mckinsey/featured%20insights/middle%20east%20and%20africa/realizing%20the%20potential%20of%20africas%20economies/mgi-lions-on-the-move-2-full-report-september-2016v2.pdf

79. As an example, see Matthew Melchiorre, *The Unintended Consequences of Italy's Labour Laws: How Extensive Labour Regulation Distorts the Italian Economy*, Institute of Economic Affairs, 2013: https://onlinelibrary.wiley.com/doi/10.1111/ecaf.12012

80. David Neumark et al., *Myth or Measurement: What Does the New Minimum Wage Research Say about Minimum Wages and Job Losses in the United States?*, National Bureau of Economic Research, January 2021: https://www.nber.org/papers/w28388?utm_campaign=ntwh&utm_medium=email&utm_source=ntwg2

81. Daniel Aaronson et al., Product Market Evidence on the Employment Effects of the Minimum Wage, Federal Reserve Bank of Chicago, 2003: https://www.chicagofed.org/publications/working-papers/2003/2003-17

82. Walter Williams, *South Africa's War Against Capitalism* (New York: Praeger, 1989)

83. Charles Lane, *Puerto Rico's crisis illustrates the risks of minimum wage hikes*, Washington Post, July 8, 2015: https://www.washingtonpost.com/opinions/puerto-ricos-lesson-for-the-mainland/2015/07/08/24e63970-25ad-11e5-b77f-eb13a215f593_story.html

84. *Ibid*, p. 58

85. Simeon Djankov et al., *Business regulations and poverty*, Economic Letters, 2018: https://econpapers.repec.org/article/eeeecolet/v_3a165_3ay_3a2018_3ai_3ac_3ap_3a82-87.htm

86. Timothy Besley et al., *Can Labor Regulation Hinder Economic Performance? Evidence from India*, The Quarterly Journal of Economics, February 2004: https://www.jstor.org/stable/25098678

87. Norman Loayza et al., The Composition of Growth Matters for Poverty Alleviation, The World Bank Group, December 2006: https://documents1.worldbank.org/curated/en/130351468140954757/pdf/wps4077.pdf

88. *Ibid*.

89. Romain Duval et al., *Labor Market Reform Options to Boost Employment in South Africa*, The IMF, June 11, 2021: https://www.imf.org/en/Publications/WP/Issues/2021/06/11/Labor-Market-Reform-Options-to-Boost-Employment-in-South-Africa-460735

CHAPTER 6

1. Max Roser (2013) - "Economic Growth". *Published online at OurWorldInData.org*. Retrieved from: 'https://ourworldindata.org/economic-growth' [Online Resource]

2. McKinsey Global Institute, *Lions on the move: the progress and potential of African economies*, p. 1-3 and p. 12

3. Daron Acemoglu et al., *An African Success Story: Botswana*, July 11, 2001: https://economics.mit.edu/files/284

4. William Easterly, *The White Man's Burden: Why the West's Efforts to Aid the Rest Have Done So Much Ill and So Little Good* (New York: Penguin Press, 2014)

5. See Fraser Institute, *Economic Freedom of the World, Annual Report 2021*, and World Bank, *Ease of Doing Business*, 2020

6. Gervase Maipose et al., Institutional Dynamics of Sustained Rapid Economic Growth with Limited Impact on Poverty Reduction, UNRISD, January 2008: https://www.unrisd.org/80256B3C005BCCF9/(httpAuxPages)/4365C57157F8EF16C1257AEF00525641/$file/Botswana%20Maipose%20web.pdf

7. Share of population living with less than $1.90 and $3.20 per day, 1981 to 2019: https://ourworldindata.org/grapher/share-of-population-living-with-less-than-190-and-320-per-day?country=~BWA

8. South African History Online, *Rwanda*: https://www.sahistory.org.za/place/rwanda

9. Annual growth of GDP per capita, 1961 to 2020: https://ourworldindata.org/grapher/gdp-per-capita-growth?tab=chart&country=RWA

10. The World Bank, *Tariff rate, applied, simple mean, all products (%) – Rwanda*: https://data.worldbank.org/indicator/TM.TAX.MRCH.SM.AR.ZS?locations=RW

11. Fraser Institute, *Economic Freedom*, Rwanda

12. OECD, *Rwanda*: https://www.oecd.org/countries/rwanda/38562991.pdf

13. The World Bank, *GDP growth (annual %) – Rwanda*: https://data.worldbank.org/indicator/NY.GDP.MKTP.KD.ZG?locations=RW

14. OECD, *Rwanda*: https://www.oecd.org/countries/rwanda/38562991.pdf

15. History World, *History of Uganda*: http://www.historyworld.net/wrldhis/plaintexthistories.asp?historyid=ad22

16. Economic Policy Research Centre, Uganda, *Liberalisation and the growth paradox in Uganda*: https://eprcug.org/blog/liberalisation-and-the-growth-paradox-in-uganda/

17. Share of population living in poverty by national poverty lines, 1992 to 2016: https://ourworldindata.org/grapher/share-of-population-living-in-poverty-by-national-poverty-lines?tab=chart&country=UGA

18. Human Rights Watch, *Democratic Republic of the Congo, Events of 2020*: https://www.hrw.org/world-report/2021/country-chapters/democratic-republic-congo

19. Andrew Walder, *China Under Mao: A Revolution Derailed* (Harvard University Press: 2015)

20. China.org.cn, *Xiaogang Village, birthplace of rural reform, moves on*, December 15, 2008: http://www.china.org.cn/china/features/content_16955209_4.htm

21. The World Bank, *Tariff rate, applied, weighted mean, all products (%) – China*: https://data.worldbank.org/indicator/TM.TAX.MRCH.WM.AR.ZS?locations=CN

22. Jack Goodman, *Has China Lifted 100 million People out of Poverty?*, BBC Reality Check, February 28, 2020: https://www.bbc.co.uk/news/56213271

23. OECD, *Revenue Statistics in Asia and the Pacific 2021 – China*: https://www.oecd.org/tax/tax-policy/revenue-statistics-asia-and-pacific-china.pdf. For statistics on social expenditure, see OECD, Society at a Glance 2016: https://www.oecd-ilibrary.org/social-issues-migration-health/society-at-a-glance-2016/social-spending_soc_glance-2016-19-en;jsessionid=Nt4jxYtItOfYJwQxRYJvh3Zr.ip-10-240-5-87

24. The World Bank, *General government final consumption expenditure (% of GDP) – China*: https://data.worldbank.org/indicator/NE.CON.GOVT.ZS?end=2019&locations=CN&start=1960&view=chart

25. OECD, *Challenges for China's Public Spending – Where the money is going: a reorientation towards human development is needed*: https://www.oecd.org/economy/surveys/challengesforchinaspublicspending-wherethemoneyisgoingareorientationtowardshumandevelopmentisneeded.htm

26. Koen Caminada et al., *Relative income poverty rates and poverty alleviation via tax/benefit systems in 49 LIS-countries, 1967-2016*, LIS Working Paper, February 2019: http://www.lisdatacenter.org/wps/liswps/761.pdf

27. Artatrana Ratha et al., *Does an Undervalued Currency Promote Growth? Evidence from China*, St. Cloud State University, 2008: https://repository.stcloudstate.edu/cgi/viewcontent.cgi?article=1014&context=econ_wps

28. Atif Ansar et al., *Does Infrastructure Investment Lead to Economic Growth or Economic Fragility? Evidence from China*, Oxford Review of Economic Policy, September 6, 2016: https://papers.ssrn.com/sol3/papers.cfm?abstract_id=2834326

29. Yasheng Huang, *China could learn from India's slow and quiet rise*, Financial Times, January 23, 2006: https://www.ft.com/content/e4462190-8c42-11da-9efb-0000779e2340

30. Yi Huang et al., *Local Crowding-Out in China*, The Journal of Finance, July 2020: https://onlinelibrary.wiley.com/doi/10.1111/jofi.12966

31. Nicholas Lardy, *Markets over Mao: The Rise of Private Business in China* (Peterson Institute for International Economics, 2014)

32. Kavita Rao, *Tax System Reform in India*, Initiative for Policy Dialogue, 2009: https://policydialogue.org/files/publications/papers/ch4_M_Govinda_Rao__R_Kavita_Rao.pdf

33. *Ibid*

34. Legatum Institute, *Global Index of Economic Openness*, 2019

35. Sriram Balasubramanian, *Sustaining India's growth miracle requires increased attention to inequality of opportunity*, Center for Economic Policy and Research, March 12, 2021: https://voxeu.org/article/sustaining-india-s-growth-miracle-requires-increased-attention-inequality-opportunity

36. Swaminathan Aiyar, *Twenty-Five Years of Indian Economic Reform*, Cato Institute, 2016: https://www.cato.org/policy-analysis/twenty-five-years-indian-economic-reform

37. Rakesh Kochnar, *In the Pandemic, India's middle class shrinks and poverty spreads while China sees smaller changes*, Pew Research Center, March 18, 2021: https://www.pewresearch.org/fact-tank/2021/03/18/in-the-pandemic-indias-middle-class-shrinks-and-poverty-spreads-while-china-sees-smaller-changes/

38. Nirupam Bajpai et al., *The Progress of Policy Reform and Variations in Performance at the Sub-National Level in India*, Columbia Academic Commons, 1999: https://academiccommons.columbia.edu/doi/10.7916/D81V5MT2

39. Timothy Besley et al., *Can Labor Regulation Hinder Economic Performance? Evidence from India*, The Quarterly Journal of Economics, 2004

40. Rana Hasan et al., *Trade Liberalization, Labor-Market Institutions, and Poverty Reduction: Evidence from Indian States*: https://sites.ualberta.ca/~ural/files/HMU_IPF_2007.pdf

41. Swaminathan Aiyar, Socialism Kills: The Human Cost of Delayed Economic Reform in India, Cato Institute, 2009

42. Risk & Compliance Portal, *India Corruption Report*, August 2020: https://www.ganintegrity.com/portal/country-profiles/india/

43. The World Bank, *General government final consumption expenditure (% of GDP) – India*: https://data.worldbank.org/indicator/NE.CON.GOVT.ZS?end=2019&locations=IN&name_desc=false&start=1960&view=chart

44. The Economist, *Private education is booming in new markets and new forms*, April 13, 2019: https://www.economist.com/special-report/2019/04/11/private-education-is-booming-in-new-markets-and-new-forms

45. Koen Caminada et al., *Relative income poverty rates and poverty alleviation via tax/benefit systems in 49 LIS-countries, 1967-2016*, LIS Working Paper, February 2019

46. Asia Pacific Curriculum, *Vietnam After the War*: https://asiapacificcurriculum.ca/learning-module/vietnam-after-war

47. The World Bank, *Climbing the Ladder: Poverty Reduction and Shared Prosperity in Vietnam*, 2018: https://openknowledge.worldbank.org/bitstream/handle/10986/29684/124916-WP-PULIC-P161323-VietnamPovertyUpdateReportENG.pdf?sequence=1&isAllowed=y

48. Peter Vanham, *The story of Viet Nam's economic miracle*, World Economic Forum, September 11, 2018: https://www.weforum.org/agenda/2018/09/how-vietnam-became-an-economic-miracle/

49. *Ibid.*

50. OECD, *Foreign Direct Investment Regulatory Restrictiveness Index*, 1997 and 2020

51. Brian McCaig, *Exporting out of poverty: Provincial poverty in Vietnam and U.S. market access*, Journal of International Economics, 2011

52. Fraser Institute, *Economic Freedom*, Chile

53. Paul Roberts and Karen Araujo, The Capitalist Revolution in Latin America (New York: Oxford University Press, 1997), p. 37

54. *Share of population living in poverty by national poverty lines, 1987 to 2017*: https://ourworldindata.org/grapher/share-of-population-living-in-poverty-by-national-poverty-lines?tab=chart&country=CHL

55. The World Bank, *Poverty & Equity Brief, Latin America & the Caribbean, Chile*, April 2020: https://databank.worldbank.org/data/download/poverty/33EF03BB-9722-4AE2-ABC7-AA2972D68AFE/Global_POVEQ_CHL.pdf

56. José Piñera, *How We Privatized Social Security in Chile, Foundation for Economic Education*, July 1997: https://fee.org/articles/how-we-privatized-social-security-in-chile/

57. The World Bank, *GDP per capita, PPP (current international $) – Lithuania, Georgia, Romania, Estonia, 1990-2020*: https://data.worldbank.org/indicator/NY.GDP.PCAP.PP.CD?locations=LT-GE-RO-EE

58. Britannica, *Post-Soviet Russia*: https://www.britannica.com/place/Russia/Post-Soviet-Russia

59. Paul Belien, *Walking on water: how to do it*, The Brussels Journal, 2005: https://www.brusselsjournal.com/node/202

60. The World Bank, *GDP per capita, PPP (current international $) – Lithuania, Georgia, Romania, Estonia, 1990-2020*: https://data.worldbank.org/indicator/NY.GDP.PCAP.PP.CD?locations=LT-GE-RO-EE

61. Daniel Bunn et al., *International Tax Competitiveness Index, 2020*, Tax Foundation

62. Trading Economics, *Romania – Poverty Gap At $5.50 A Day (2011 PPP) (%)*: https://tradingeconomics.com/romania/poverty-gap-at-$5-50-a-day-2011-ppp-percent-wb-data.html

63. Fraser Institute, *Economic Freedom*, 2020, Romania

64. The World Bank, *GDP per capita, PPP (current international $) – Lithuania, Georgia, Romania, Estonia, 1990-2020*: https://data.worldbank.org/indicator/NY.GDP.PCAP.PP.CD?locations=LT-GE-RO-EE

65. Daniel Bunn et al., *International Tax Competitiveness Index, 2020*, Tax Foundation

66. World Bank, *Doing Business*, 2020: https://www.doingbusiness.org/en/rankings

67. World Bank Group, *Georgia: from Reformer to Performer*, 2018: https://documents1.worldbank.org/curated/en/496731525097717444/pdf/GEO-SCD-04-24-04272018.pdf

68. Eurostat, *Mean and median incomes by household type – EU-SILC and ECHP surveys*: https://appsso.eurostat.ec.europa.eu/nui/show.do?dataset=ilc_di04

69. OECD, *Hourly Earnings (MEI)*: https://stats.oecd.org/Index.aspx?DataSetCode=EAR_MEI

70. Trading Economics, *New Zealand Interest Rate*: https://tradingeconomics.com/new-zealand/interest-rate

CHAPTER 7

1. Camelia Minoiu et al., *Development Aid and Economic Growth: A Positive Long-Run Relation*, IMF Working Paper, 2009: https://www.imf.org/external/pubs/ft/wp/2009/wp09118.pdf

2. Sandrina Moreira, *Evaluating the Impact of Foreign Aid on Economic Growth: A Cross-Country Study*, Journal of Economic Development, 2005

3. Elizabeth Adusei, *The impact of Foreign Aid on Economic Growth in Sub-Saharan Africa: The mediating role of institutions*, MPRA, 2020: https://mpra.ub.uni-muenchen.de/104561/

4. Sebastian Galiani, *The Effect of Aid on Growth: Evidence from a Quasi-Experiment*, National Bureau of Economic Research, 2016: https://www.nber.org/system/files/working_papers/w22164/w22164.pdf

5. Albrecht Ritschl, *The Marshall Plan, 1948-1951*, Economic History Association: https://eh.net/encyclopedia/the-marshall-plan-1948-1951/

6. The Heritage Foundation, U.S Aid to the Developing World: A Free-Market Agenda, Tyler Cowen, *The Marshall Plan: Myths and Realities*, 1983: https://d101vc9winf8ln.cloudfront.net/documents/28244/original/Marshall_Plan.pdf?1527192058

7. David Henderson, *German Economic Miracle*, The Library of Economics and Liberty: https://www.econlib.org/library/Enc/GermanEconomicMiracle.html

8. Correlli Barnett, *The Lost Victory: British Dreams, British Reality, 1945-1950* (London: Macmillan, 1995)

9. Albrecht Ritschl, *The Marshall Plan, 1948-1951*, Economic History Association

10. Ramesh Durbarry et al., *New Evidence of the Impact of Foreign Aid on Economic Growth*, CREDIT Research Paper: https://www.nottingham.ac.uk/credit/documents/papers/98-08.pdf

11. Thian-Hee Yiew et al., *Does foreign aid contribute to or impede economic growth*, Journal of International Studies, 2018: https://jois.eu/files/2_493_Yiew_Lau.pdf

12. David Dollar et al., *Aid, Policies, and Growth*, Available at SSRN, 1997: https://papers.ssrn.com/sol3/papers.cfm?abstract_id=569252

13. William Easterly, The White Man's Burden (Penguin Press, 2006), p. 35

14. Raghuram Rajan et al., *Aid and Growth: What does the Cross-Country Evidence Really Show?*, IMF Working Paper, 2005: https://www.imf.org/external/pubs/ft/wp/2005/wp05127.pdf

15. Sikiru Babalola et al., *Foreign Aid and Economic Growth in West Africa: Examining the Roles of Institutions*, International Economic Journal, 2020: https://www.tandfonline.com/doi/abs/10.1080/10168737.2020.1780292?journalCode=riej20

16. Axel Dreher et al., *Aid and growth: New evidence using an excludable instrument*, Canadian Journal of Economics, September 7, 2020: https://onlinelibrary.wiley.com/doi/full/10.1111/caje.12455

17. Albimann MM, *What are the Impacts of Foreign Aid to the Economic Growth? Time Series Analysis with New Evidence from Tanzania*, Business and Economics Journal, 2016: https://www.hilarispublisher.com/open-access/what-are-the-impact-of-foreign-aid-to-the-economic-growth-time-seriesanalysis-with-new-evidence-from-tanzania-2151-6219-1000208.pdf

18. Human Rights Watch, *Democratic Republic of the Congo, Events of 2020*

19. Benjamin Powell, *Markets created a pot of gold in Ireland*, Cato Institute, April 15, 2003: https://www.cato.org/commentary/markets-created-pot-gold-ireland

20. Dambisa Moyo, Dead Aid: Why Aid is Not Working and How There is Another Way for Africa (Macmillan, 2009)

CHAPTER 8

1. Ethan Ilzetzki et al., *How Big (Small) Are Fiscal Multipliers?*, National Bureau of Economic Research, 2010: https://www.nber.org/papers/w16479

2. Congressional Budget Office, *The Macroeconomic and Budgetary Effects of Federal Investment*, June 2016, p. 9: https://www.cbo.gov/sites/default/files/114th-congress-2015-2016/reports/51628-Federal_Investment.pdf

3. Nihal Bayraktar et al., *How Can Public Spending Help You Grow? An Empirical Analysis for Developing Countries*, Bulletin of Economic Research, 2012: https://onlinelibrary.wiley.com/doi/full/10.1111/j.1467-8586.2012.00473.x

4. Recall the study mentioned earlier whose results found that the optimal, growth-boosting size of government is around 25 percent of GDP.

5. Andrew Warner, *Public Investment as an Engine of Growth*, IMF Working Paper, 2014: https://www.imf.org/external/pubs/ft/wp/2014/wp14148.pdf

6. David Canning et al., *Infrastructure, Long-Run Economic Growth and Causality Tests for Cointegrated Panels*, The Manchester School, 2008: https://onlinelibrary.wiley.com/doi/abs/10.1111/j.1467-9957.2008.01073.x

7. Xinshen Diao et al., *Mechanization in Ghana: Emerging demand, and the search for alternative supply models*, Food Policy, 2014: https://www.sciencedirect.com/science/article/pii/S0306919214000876

8. Alma Kudebayeva et al., *A Decade of Poverty Reduction in Kazakhstan 2001-2009: Growth and/or Redistribution*, Journal of International Development, 2017: https://onlinelibrary.wiley.com/doi/10.1002/jid.3278

9. Shi Li, *Poverty Reduction and Effects of Pro-poor Policies in Rural China*, China & World Economy, 2014: https://onlinelibrary.wiley.com/doi/full/10.1111/j.1749-124X.2014.12060.x

10. Russel Bither-Terry, *Reducing Poverty Intensity: What Alternative Poverty Measures Reveal About the Impact of Brazil's Bolsa Família*, Latin American Politics and Society, 2014: https://onlinelibrary.wiley.com/doi/full/10.1111/j.1548-2456.2014.00252.x

11. United Nations, Base de datos de inversion social en América Latina y el Caribe: https://observatoriosocial.cepal.org/inversion/en/countries

12. Anthony Hall, *Brazil's Bolsa Família: A Double-Edged Sword?*, Development and Change, 2008: https://onlinelibrary.wiley.com/doi/10.1111/j.1467-7660.2008.00506.x

13. Mark Weisbrot et al., *Did NAFTA Help Mexico? An Update After 23 Years*, Centre for Economic and Policy Research, 2017: https://cepr.net/images/stories/reports/nafta-mexico-update-2017-03.pdf?v=2&__cf_chl_jschl_tk__=pmd_r6jJMXmnlT0QTTj8gr.D2kIIZHqXJX3dI5O10STo0Ss-1632517383-0-gqNtZGzNAlCjcnBszQfl

14. Silvia Borzutzky, *Anti-Poverty Politics in Chile: A Preliminary Assessment of the Chile Solidario Program*, Poverty and Public Policy, 2012: https://onlinelibrary.wiley.com/doi/10.2202/1944-2858.1005

15. Nizar Jouini et al., *Fiscal Policy, Income Redistribution, and Poverty Reduction*, The review of income and wealth, 2018: https://onlinelibrary.wiley.com/doi/10.1111/roiw.12372

16. Stephen Younger et al., *Fiscal Incidence in Ghana*, Review of Development Economics, 2017: https://onlinelibrary.wiley.com/doi/full/10.1111/rode.12299

17. M Anne Hill et al., *Underclass behaviours in the United States: measurement and analysis of determinants*, Center for the Study of Business and Government, 1993: https://www.worldcat.org/title/underclass-behaviors-in-the-united-states-measurement-and-analysis-of-determinants/oclc/31505949

18. Robert Rector et al., *Universal Basic Income Harms Recipients and Increases Dependence on Government*, The Heritage Foundation, 2018: https://www.heritage.org/sites/default/files/2018-02/IB4817.pdf

19. Pirmin Fessler et al., *Private wealth across European countries: the role of income, inheritance and the welfare state*, European Central Bank, Working Paper Series, 2015: https://www.ecb.europa.eu/pub/pdf/scpwps/ecbwp1847.en.pdf

20. Artur Ribaj et al., *The impact of savings on economic growth in a developing country (the case of Kosovo)*, Journal of Innovation and Entrepreneurship, 2021: https://innovation-entrepreneurship.springeropen.com/articles/10.1186/s13731-020-00140-6

21. Kafayat Amusa et al., *Savings and Economic Growth in Botswana: An Analysis Using Bounds Testing Approach to Cointegration*, Journal of Economics and Behavioural Studies, 2013: https://core.ac.uk/download/pdf/288022667.pdf

22. Piotr Misztal, *The Relationship Between Savings and Economic Growth in Countries with Different Levels of Economic Development*, Financial Internet Quarterly, 2011: https://www.econstor.eu/obitstream/10419/66731/1/670173894.pdf

23. Just Facts: https://www.justfacts.com/income_wealth_poverty#introductory

24. Adam Thomas et al., For Richer or for Poorer: Marriage as an Antipoverty Strategy, Brookings Institution, 2002: https://www.brookings.edu/articles/for-richer-or-for-poorer-marriage-as-an-antipoverty-strategy/

25. Ron Haskins et al., *Work and Marriage: The Way to End Poverty and Welfare*, The Brookings Institution, September 2003: https://www.brookings.edu/wp-content/uploads/2016/06/pb28.pdf

26. Richard Fording et al., *The Historical Impact of Welfare Programs: Evidence from the American States*, Policy Studies Journal, 2007: https://onlinelibrary.wiley.com/doi/full/10.1111/j.1541-0072.2007.00206.x

27. Amie Shei et al., *The impact of Brazil's Bolsa Familia conditional transfer program on children's health care utilization and health outcomes*, BMC International Health and Human Rights, 2014: https://www.ncbi.nlm.nih.gov/pmc/articles/PMC4021270/

28. Testimony of Ron Haskins, Senior Fellow, Brookings Institution, Senior Consultant, Annie E. Casey Foundation, Committee on Ways and Means, 2006: https://www.brookings.edu/wp-content/uploads/2016/06/20060719-1.pdf

29. Benjamin Powell, *Markets created a pot of gold in Ireland*, Cato Institute, April 15, 2003

30. Robert Rector, *Examining the Means-tested Welfare-State: 79 Programs and $927 Billion in Annual Spending*, The Heritage Foundation, May 3, 2012: https://www.heritage.org/testimony/examining-the-means-tested-welfare-state-79-programs-and-927-billion-annual-spending

31. Karl Widerquist, *The Cost of a Full Basic Income for the United Kingdom Would be £67 billion per year (3.4% of GDP)*, Basic Income Earth Network, September 5, 2020: https://basicincome.org/news/2020/09/the-cost-of-a-full-basic-income-for-the-united-kingdom-would-be-67-billion-per-year-3-4-of-gdp/

32. Stephanie Wykstra, *Microcredit was a hugely hyped solution to global poverty. What happened?*, Vox, January 15, 2019: https://www.vox.com/future-perfect/2019/1/15/18182167/microcredit-microfinance-poverty-grameen-bank-yunus

33. BBC News, *Microcredit in Bangladesh 'helped 10 million'*, January 27, 2011: https://www.bbc.co.uk/news/business-12292108

34. Mark Skousen, *A Private-Sector Solution to Extreme Poverty, Chapter 21, Summary*, 2012: https://onlinelibrary.wiley.com/doi/10.1002/9781119196914.ch21

35. The Economist, *Indonesia's economic growth is being held back by populism*, January 19, 2019: https://www.economist.com/asia/2019/01/17/indonesias-economic-growth-is-being-held-back-by-populism

36. DollarAndSense.sg, *Debunking 3 Myths About Singapore's Wage Growth*, December 10, 2015: https://dollarsandsense.sg/debunking-3-myths-about-singapores-wage-growth/

37. Paul Krugman, *America Needs to Empower its Workers Again*, New York Times, April 12, 2021: https://www.nytimes.com/2021/04/12/opinion/us-unions-amazon.html

38. Walter Williams, *South Africa's War Against Capitalism* (New York: Praeger, 1989)

39. Stéphane Adjemian et al., *How do Labour Market Institutions affect the Link between Growth and Unemployment: the case of the European countries*, European Journal of Comparative Economics, 2010: https://ideas.repec.org/a/liu/liucej/v7y2010i2p347-371.html

40. Rachel Greszler, *Why Volkswagen Workers Should be Wary of Unionizing*, The Daily Signal, June 12, 2019: https://www.dailysignal.com/2019/06/12/why-volkswagen-workers-should-be-wary-of-unionizing/

41. Richard Vedder et al., *The economic effects of labor unions revisited*, Journal of Labor Research, March 2002, p. 127: https://link.springer.com/article/10.1007/s12122-002-1021-7

42. Caroline Banton, *Wage-Price Spiral*, Investopedia: https://www.investopedia.com/terms/w/wage-price-spiral.asp

43. Richard Vedder et al., *The economic effects of labor unions revisited*, Journal of Labor Research, March 2002

44. Ayn Rand, *Capitalism and Freedom, Notes on the History of American Free Enterprise* (New American Library, 1967)

45. Burton Folsom, *When the Telegraph Came to Michigan*, Mackinac Center for Public Policy, December 8, 1997: https://www.mackinac.org/V1997-40

46. McKinsey Global Institute, *Lions on the move: The progress and potential of African economies*, June 2010, p. 49

47. Mo Ibrahim, *Celtel's Founder on Building a Business on the World's Poorest Continent*, Harvard Business Review, 2012: https://hbr.org/2012/10/celtels-founder-on-building-a-business-on-the-worlds-poorest-continent

48. The Economist, *Wanted: a champion for privatisation*, October 28, 2006: https://www.economist.com/leaders/2006/10/26/wanted-a-champion-for-privatisation

49. McKinsey Global Institute, *Lions on the move: The progress and potential of African economies*, June 2010, p. 49

50. Sudeshna Banerjee, *Private Provision of Infrastructure in Emerging Markets: Do Institutions Matter?*, Development Policy Review, 2006

51. Transportation Research Board, *Passenger-Friendly Airports: Another Reason for Airport Privatization*, 1999: https://trid.trb.org/view/680630

52. International Transport Forum, *Liberalisation of Air Travel*, Research Report, 2019: https://www.itf-oecd.org/sites/default/files/docs/liberalisation_air_transport.pdf

53. *Competition Policy for Shared Prosperity and Inclusive Growth*, World Bank Group, 2017, p. 37

54. *Ibid.*

55. Stephen Malpezzi, *Housing Prices, Externalities, and Regulation, in U.S. Metropolitan Areas*, Journal of Housing Research, November 1996: https://papers.ssrn.com/sol3/papers.cfm?abstract_id=9173

56. Edward Glaeser et al., *Why Is Manhattan So Expensive? Regulation and the Rise in Housing Prices*, The Journal of Law and Economics, October 2005: https://www.journals.uchicago.edu/doi/abs/10.1086/429979

57. The Council of Economic Advisers, *The State of Homelessness in America*, September 2019: https://www.nhipdata.org/local/upload/file/The-State-of-Homelessness-in-America.pdf

58. Cavalcanti T., *On the determinants of slum formation*, Economic Journal, 2019: https://www.repository.cam.ac.uk/handle/1810/279728

59. Alves, G., *Determinants of Slum Formation: The Role of Local Politics and Policies*, SCIOTECA, 2018: https://scioteca.caf.com/handle/123456789/1158

60. Sahil Ghandi et al., *Decline of Rental Housing in India: A Case Study of Mumbai*, Marron Institute of Urban Management, 2014: https://marroninstitute.nyu.edu/uploads/content/Decline_of_Rental_Housing_in_India.pdf

61. The World Bank, *Natural Hazards, Unnatural Disasters: The Economics of Effective Prevention*, 2010

62. McKinsey Global Institute, *Lions on the move: The progress and potential of African economies*, June 2010, p. 21

63. The Economist, *Indonesia's economic growth is being held back by populism*, January 19, 2019

64. Caroline Hoxby, *School Choice and School Productivity, Could School Choice Be a Tide that Lifts all Boats?*, National Bureau of Economic Research, 2003: https://www.nber.org/system/files/chapters/c10091/c10091.pdf

65. Corey Iacono, *3 Reasons to Support School Choice*, Foundation for Economic Education, January 26, 2015: https://fee.org/articles/3-reasons-to-support-school-choice/

66. The Economist, *Free to choose, to learn*, May 5, 2007: https://www.economist.com/international/2007/05/03/free-to-choose-and-learn

67. James Tooley et al., *School Choice in Lagos State*, DFID Nigeria, January 6, 2014: https://assets.publishing.service.gov.uk/media/57a089b940f0b652dd000394/61517_Final_Summary_Lagos_School_Choice.pdf

68. The Economist, *Private schools that educate 50% of Indian children are folding*, January 7, 2021: https://www.economist.com/asia/2021/01/07/private-schools-that-educate-50-of-indian-children-are-folding

69. Karthik Muralidharan et al., *Public and Private Schools in Rural India*, September 1, 2007: https://scholar.harvard.edu/files/kremer/files/public_and_private_schools_in_rural_india_final_pre-publication.pdf

70. The Economist, *Private schools that educate 50% of Indian children are folding*, January 7, 2021

71. Richard Frank et al., *Pricing, Patent Loss and the Market For Pharmaceuticals*, Southern Economic Journal, 1993: https://www.researchgate.net/publication/5191778_Pricing_Patent_Loss_and_the_Market_For_Pharmaceuticals

72. UNICEF, *Long-Lasting Insecticidal Nets: Supply Update*, UNICEF Supply Division, March 2020: https://www.unicef.org/supply/media/2361/file/Long-lasting-insecticidal-nets-market-and-supply-update.pdf

73. John Alionby, *Africa's anti-malaria net makers face a tough market*, Financial Times, April 24, 2016: https://www.ft.com/content/212189c2-f83c-11e5-96db-fc683b5e52db

74. Deepak Lal, Bring Back DDT, Cato Institute, April 26, 2016: https://www.cato.org/commentary/bring-back-ddt. See also, Max Roser and Hannah Ritchie (2019) - "Malaria". *Published online at OurWorldInData.org*. Retrieved from: 'https://ourworldindata.org/malaria' [Online Resource]

75. WSJ Opinion, *DDT Saves Lives*, November 8, 2005: https://www.wsj.com/articles/SB113141500661590763

76. Ivaldi et al., *Competition Policy for Shared Prosperity and Inclusive Growth*, World Bank Group, 2017, chapter 3

77. Tarun Khanna et al., *Narayana Hrudayalaya Heart Hospital: Cardiac Care for the Poor (A)*, Harvard Business School: https://www.hbs.edu/faculty/Pages/item.aspx?num=32452

78. Travis Klavohn et al., *The Medical Cartel is Keeping Health Care Costs High*, Foundation for Economic Education, August 6, 2017: https://fee.org/articles/the-medical-cartel-is-keeping-health-care-costs-high/

79. The World Bank, *Physicians (per 1,000 people) – United States, OECD Members*, 1960-2017: https://data.worldbank.org/indicator/SH.MED.PHYS.ZS?locations=US-OE

80. David Cutler et al., *Managed Care and the Growth of Medical Expenditures*, National Bureau of Economic Research, August 1997: https://www.nber.org/system/files/working_papers/w6140/w6140.pdf

81. James Bartholomew, *The Welfare of Nations, In search of the best healthcare system in the world* (Biteback Publishing, 2015)

82. Anna Gorter et al., *Improving access to reproductive care and child health care services in developing countries: Are competitive voucher schemes an option?*, Journal of International Development, 2007: https://www.researchgate.net/publication/23992582_Improving_access_to_reproductive_and_child_health_services_in_developing_countries_Are_competitive_voucher_schemes_an_option

83. Nicole Bellows et al., *Systematic Review: the use of vouchers for reproductive health services in developing countries*, Trop Med Int Health, 2010: https://pubmed.ncbi.nlm.nih.gov/21044235/

84. OECD, *Fiscal Decentralisation and Inclusive Growth: Fiscal Decentralisation and the efficiency of public service delivery*, 2018: https://www.oecd-ilibrary.org/governance/fiscal-decentralisation-and-inclusive-growth/fiscal-decentralisation-and-the-efficiency-of-public-service-delivery_9789264302488-11-en

85. Guangrong Ma et al., *Fiscal Decentralisation and Local Economic Growth: Evidence from a Fiscal Reform in China*, Fiscal Studies, 2017

86. Su Dinh Thanh et al., *Fiscal Decentralization and Economic Growth of Vietnamese Provinces: The Role of Local Public Governance*, Annals of Public and Cooperative Economics, September 2019

CHAPTER 9

1. Trading Economics, *Inflation Rate*: https://tradingeconomics.com/country-list/inflation-rate

2. Stephen Cecchetti et al., *The real effects of debt*, Bank of International Settlements, September 2011: https://www.bis.org/publ/othp16.pdf

3. Carmen Reinhart et al., *Growth in a Time of Debt*, American Economic Review, 2010: https://scholar.harvard.edu/files/rogoff/files/growth_in_time_debt_aer.pdf

4. Goohoon Kwon et al., *Public Debt, Money Supply, and Inflation: A Cross-Country Study*, IMF Staff Papers, 2009: https://ideas.repec.org/a/pal/imfstp/v56y2009i3p476-515.html

5. José da Veiga et al., *Public Debt, Economic Growth and Inflation in African Economies*, South African Journal of Economics, 2015: https://onlinelibrary.wiley.com/doi/full/10.1111/saje.12104

6. Julia Kagan, *Deflationary Spiral*, Investopedia, August 27, 2021: https://www.investopedia.com/terms/d/deflationary-spiral.asp

7. Steven Kennedy, *Australia's response to the global financial crisis*, Australian Government: The Treasury, June 24, 2009: https://treasury.gov.au/speech/australias-response-to-the-global-financial-crisis

8. Guy Pfefferman, *Public Expenditure in Latin America: Effects on Poverty*, World Bank discussion paper, 1987. For poverty statistics, see Dominique van de Walle, *Poverty and Inequality in Latin America and the Caribbean during the 70s and 80s: An Overview of the Evidence*, LATHR, September 1991

9. William Easterly et al., *The macroeconomics of public sector deficits: a synthesis*, World Bank Policy Research Papers, 1991: https://ideas.repec.org/p/wbk/wbrwps/775.html

10. Matthew Johnston, *Understanding the Downfall of Greece's Economy*, Investopedia, June 23, 2021: https://www.investopedia.com/articles/investing/070115/understanding-downfall-greeces-economy.asp

11. Jeffrey Sachs et al., *Sources of Slow Growth in African Economies*, Journal of African Economies, 1997, p. 348

12. David Faulkner et al., *Policy Change and Economic Growth: A Case Study for South Africa*, Commission on Growth and Development. See also, Ashok Bundia et al., *Potential Output and total Factor Productivity Growth in Post-Apartheid South Africa*, IMF Working Paper, 2003: https://econpapers.repec.org/paper/imfimfwpa/2003_2f178.htm

13. Alberto Alesina et al., *The Output Effect of Fiscal Consolidation*, National Bureau of Economic Research, August 2012: https://www.nber.org/system/files/working_papers/w18336/w18336.pdf

CHAPTER 10

1. James Purtill, *$26 a month: Ethiopians are being paid world's lowest wages to make your Calvin Kleins*, ABC, May 9, 2019: https://www.abc.net.au/triplej/programs/hack/ethiopian-garment-workers-are-being-paid-worlds-lowest-wages/11098232

2. Drusilla Brown et al., *The Effects of Multinational Production on Wages and Working Conditions in Developing Countries*, National Bureau of Economic Research, February 2004: https://www.nber.org/system/files/chapters/c9541/c9541.pdf

3. Benjamin Powell, *In Défense of Sweatshops*, The Library of Economics and Liberty: https://www.econlib.org/library/Columns/y2008/Powellsweatshops.html

4. World Bank Group, *Evidence-Insights-Policy*: https://thedocs.worldbank.org/en/doc/395561556138139819-0050022019/original/5HighgrowthentrepreneursWeb.pdf

5. McKinsey Global Institute, *Lions on the Move II: Realising the Potential of Africa's Economies*, September 2016, p. 63

6. Amy Quandt et al., *Mobile phone use is associated with higher smallholder agricultural productivity in Tanzania, East Africa*, Plos One, August 2020: https://journals.plos.org/plosone/article?id=10.1371/journal.pone.0237337

7. Olaniyi Evans, *Digital Agriculture: Mobile Phones, Internet & Agricultural Development in Africa*, MPRA, 2018: https://core.ac.uk/download/pdf/211629343.pdf

8. Rob Matheson, *Study: Mobile-money services lift Kenyans out of poverty*, MIT News, December 8, 2016: https://news.mit.edu/2016/mobile-money-kenyans-out-poverty-1208

9. *Ibid.*

10. The Economist, *Mobile phones are transforming Africa*, December 10, 2016: https://www.economist.com/middle-east-and-africa/2016/12/10/mobile-phones-are-transforming-africa

11. *Ibid.*

12. Karol Boudreaux, *Seeds of Hope: Agricultural Technologies and Poverty Alleviation in Rural South Africa*, Mercatus Center, August 22, 2006: https://www.mercatus.org/publications/entrepreneurship/seeds-hope-agricultural-technologies-and-poverty-alleviation-rural

13. J H Humphrey et al., *Vitamin A deficiency and attributable mortality among under 5-year-olds*, Bull World Health Organ, 1992: https://pubmed.ncbi.nlm.nih.gov/1600583/

14. Grain, *Don't get fooled again! Unmasking two decades of lies about Golden Rice*, November 21, 2018: https://grain.org/en/article/6067-don-t-get-fooled-again-unmasking-two-decades-of-lies-about-golden-rice

15. Robin McKie, *Block on GM rice 'has cost millions of lives and led to child blindness'*, The Guardian, October 26, 2019: https://www.theguardian.com/environment/2019/oct/26/gm-golden-rice-delay-cost-millions-of-lives-child-blindness

16. Xinshen Diao et al., *Mechanization in Ghana: Emerging demand, and the search for alternative supply models*, Food Policy, October 2014: https://www.sciencedirect.com/science/article/pii/S0306919214000876

CPSIA information can be obtained
at www.ICGtesting.com
Printed in the USA
LVHW102053010422
714807LV00012B/353